MILITARY HISTORY

OF

WATERVILLE, MAINE

Including the Names and Record, So Far as Known, of All Soldiers from Waterville, in the

Several Wars of the Republic;

a Portion of the Records of the

Waterville Monument Association,

and a Sketch of

W. S. Heath Post, No. 14, G.A.R.

Brevet Brig. General Isaac S. Bangs

HERITAGE BOOKS
2024

HERITAGE BOOKS

AN IMPRINT OF HERITAGE BOOKS, INC.

Books, CDs, and more—Worldwide

For our listing of thousands of titles see our website at
www.HeritageBooks.com

A Facsimile Reprint
Published 2024 by
HERITAGE BOOKS, INC.
Publishing Division
5810 Ruatan Street
Berwyn Heights, MD 20740

Copyright © 1902 Dennis M. Bangs

Originally published:
AUGUSTA
Kennebec Journal Print
1902

— Publisher's Notice —
In reprints such as this, it is often not possible to remove blemishes from the original. We feel the contents of this book warrant its reissue despite these blemishes and hope you will agree and read it with pleasure.

International Standard Book Number
Paperbound: 978-0-7884-3128-9

THE MILITARY HISTORY OF WATERVILLE.

Its record in the Revolution—the War of 1812—The Aroostook War—the Mexican, Spanish and Philippine Wars, with rosters of soldiers who have served in each, military records, etc.—also sketch of the Waterville Soldiers' Monument Association and of W. S. Heath Post, No. 14, Department of Maine, G. A. R.

By Brevet Brig. General Isaac Sparrow Bangs.

Of all the magnificent pageants this country has ever seen, from its settlement to the present year, none in point of interest can compare to the grand review of the armies of the Union on May 23 and 24, 1865.

The most causeless, cruel, bloody war in the world's history had just been brought to a triumphant close by the surrender of the army of Northern Virginia, under General Robert E. Lee, to General Grant, at Appomattox, April 9th, and the surrender of Johnston's and all confederate armies east of the Mississippi by the military convention of April 26th.

The identical flag that was lowered from the flagstaff of Fort Sumter by Major Robert Anderson April 14, 1861, was floating over Fort Sumter again, having been raised by Brevet Major General Robert Anderson on the 14th of April, 1865; the fourth anniversary to commemorate in the most fitting manner the restoration of national authority on the spot where the great rebellion was first inaugurated.

On the evening of that same day, President Lincoln had fallen a victim to the hate engendered by the war, by the bullet of John Wilkes Booth, at Ford's theatre in Washington.

May 18th, by Special Orders No. 239, war department, adjutant general's office, a grand review by General Grant, President Johnson and cabinet, was ordered of all the armies then near Washington; to take place May 23rd and 24th. These great armies had bivouacked in the streets of the capital the previous night, and when the hour arrived, the army of the Potomac led the way around the capitol, down Pennsylvania avenue, out past the reviewing stand at the White House; passing for the last time as regimental organizations before their beloved commander.

With tattered flags, faded uniforms, marks of battle and exposure; but keen-eyed, alert, bronzed, they swung along with elastic stride in close column by division; cheered by thousands who gloried in their loyalty, their victories and final triumph.

These were the men of Antietam, Fredericksburg, Gettysburg, the Wilderness and Spottsylvania, whose undaunted courage had stood between their country and ruin, between their flag and dishonor, for four long years;—the men whose exultant faces were set toward home.

The 24th brought Sherman's splendid army, who in a campaign of two thousand miles of marching and fighting had cut the confederacy in twain, and joined Grant at the Nation's capital. Sixty-five thousand bronzed veterans who had won each a blazonry for his "shield without device" at Chattanooga, Dalton, Resaca, Kenesaw, or Atlanta,—in the army of the Tennessee under Howard,—in the army of Georgia under Slocum,— in the army of the Ohio under Schofield, or in the cavalry division with Kilpatrick.

For two entire days these marching hosts filled Washington's streets; serried ranks of glistening steel with touches of color in the tattered flags they had carried for four long years and loved so well; martial music, songs, shouts of welcome, and ringing cheers filled the air with sound; while the hearts of the welcoming thousands were overflowing with gladness that peace had come at last and "come to stay."

The effect of this moving military pageant must be lost, except as an historical incident, to the generation born since the war; but to those then living it bore tremendous significance. No one can ever know, who was not then living, the tumultuous joy of the people over the close of the war and the return of the men who had saved the country.

It may well be asked by those who do not know: "If the War of the Rebellion ended with so much rejoicing, by what fanfare was it inaugurated?"

We will turn back the pages of history for four years and stand in the streets of the village of Waterville, the embryo city of to-day, just forty-one years ago. It is not the purpose of this article to describe the physical changes that man and "God hath wrought." Indeed, these have been so insidious, so gradual, and at the same time so radical, that old things have become new. Even the people are new! One wonders where the old buildings are, since one misses them,—and the old faces; just like any child who puzzles his wits to know where all the moons go.

It is impossible not to remember that the enduring quality of its buildings was then represented by a few unpretentious brick stores: the Ticonic row, Getchell block, the Noyes (Phœnix) block, the Boutelle, the Morrill, and the one " where David Webb traded," and just replaced by the Flood block. As for the others, they were more or less pretentious frames, and have been moved—no one can remember *when* or *how,* and handsome brick blocks fill their places. The old stores can be found out on back streets metamorphosed into dwellings with front piazzas, bow windows, and new paint,—"spruced up" like a widower with a second wife.

The popular resorts in the late 50s and the 60s were "the hardware store," John Caffrey's, and the gymnasium, which stood on the site of the post office block. At the gymnasium, the evening classes were popular and comprised representative men of the town; life-long friends who had "Lived and loved together through many a changing year," and stood shoulder to shoulder in support of the government and in sympathy with the soldier, through all the weary days of the tedious months, of the terrible years of the war. Among these were Edwin Noyes, Dr. Boutelle, Charles M. Morse, Jones Elden, Nathaniel and John Meader, C. R. McFadden, John and William Caffrey, W. B. Arnold, Joshua Nye, George Robinson, G. A. Phillips, J. P. Hill, William Blunt, A. A. Plaisted, Simeon Keith, E. G. Meader and I. S. Bangs; names to conjure with; of men who controlled public sentiment and stood for law and order always and everywhere.

A history of "Waterville in the war" would be incomplete without mentioning a few of the prominent older men:

Hon. D. L. Milliken, Gen. Franklin Smith, F. D. Haviland, Major Samuel Appleton, Dr. D. N. Sheldon, Dr. J. T. Champlin, John Ware, Julius Alden, William and Walter Getchell, R. B.

Dunn, John Webber, Prof. George Keeley,—noble men of wise counsels and great hearts, whose waking thoughts when conflict was joined, were always with our armies; whose "purse and pen" sustained the government and encouraged the leaders to final victory and peace.

The years in which these men lived and wrought have gone where the roses go; many have crossed the river, but the influence of their lives and their loyalty in "the times that tried men's souls," has left a fragrant memory with those that knew them.

As for the questions the solution of which was so important to the great Republic of to-day, it may be said: God wrought them out in his own way, in his own appointed time, through the Civil War, and they were settled forever.

The first rebel gun fired at Fort Sumter, April 12, 1861, roused all the latent patriotism of the North, united all parties or, better, obliterated all parties, and when the President's call of April 15th for 75,000 men was flashed over the wires, the enthusiasm was so great that a million men would have offered their services if required, and they could have been armed and fed.

In Waterville a recruiting office was opened in the office of Joshua Nye, then treasurer of the old Androscoggin and Kennebec Railroad Company, on the second floor of the Hanscom block, corner of Elm and Main streets, on the morning of April 16th, the day following the call of President Lincoln.

Charles A. Henrickson, then an undergraduate at Waterville College, was the first to sign the roll as a volunteer from Waterville, and his patriotic zeal and his exaltation as a new volunteer proved so irresistibly contagious at the college that the classes and recitations were broken up. Finally, to save the classes, the president and faculty voted to close the college temporarily.

Another recruiting office was opened on the second floor of the Plaisted building, which now stands on Charles street. This was in charge of William S. Heath, his brother Frank E. Heath, and J. H. Plaisted, who were the first to volunteer there, and each arrived at distinction in the service.

In a few days the companies were filled and began squad and company drill in our streets; were soon ordered to Augusta into camp, and on June 4th were mustered into the service of the United States as Companies G and H of the Third Maine Infantry Volunteers. Company G was commanded by Frank S. Hesseltine, with Nathaniel Hanscom 1st lieutenant and William A. Hatch 2nd lieutenant. Company H was commanded by W. S Heath, with F. E. Heath as 1st lieutenant and John R. Day as 2nd lieutenant.

O. O. Howard was appointed colonel of the regiment, and on the 5th of June he was ordered to Washington with his command, carrying with him, as Waterville's first contingent, seventy-four of her boys into the maelstrom of war.

Meantime, apprehending the embarrassment under which the general government would labor to defend itself against the organized rebellion of the South, the legislature of Maine, at an extra session called to consider and provide for the exigencies of the hour, determined to furnish the government at the earliest moment with ten regiments fully armed and equipped, from the enrolled but unarmed militia of 60,000 men, to serve for two years. This act was passed and approved April 25th.

How the men who voted for this measure expected to arm and equip these men, *they* never knew, but they *did* know it *must be done.*

Thus the regiments from the 1st to the 10th inclusive were organized by this act of the legislature, and all succeeding organizations by the general government or by its authority.

It must be borne in mind that the 1st Regiment Maine Infantry had been mustered into service for three months at Portland May 4th, and the 2nd Regiment Maine Infantry mustered at Bangor May 28th, and both sent at once to the front.

The 3rd was mustered June 5th; the 4th June 15th; the 5th June 24th; the 6th July 15th; the 7th August 21st; the 8th September 7th; the 9th September 22nd; the 10th October 4th; the 11th November 4th; the 12th November 15th; the 13th November 20th; the 14th December 11th; the 15th December 17th; the first cavalry October 19th, and six batteries; making with five companies of sharpshooters and coast guards*, 16,669 men; and of this number Waterville furnished 121 in 1861.

Waterville College furnished from its alumni and undergraduate classes the following list of patriotic young men for Com-

---

*The U. S. Government credited the State of Maine with 18,875 for the year 1861.

pany G, 3rd Maine: Charles A. Henrickson, class of 1864; William E. Brown, class of 1864; George H. Bassett, class of 1864, died in service; Atwood Crosby, class of 1864; Moses W. Young, class of 1864; E. P. Stearns, class of 1864, died in service; Frank S. Hesseltine, class of 1863; A. C. Hinds, class of 1863, died in service; Samuel Hamblen, class of 1862; Amasa Bigelow, Jr., class of 1862; J. A. Philbrook, class of 1862; William A. Hatch, class of 1861.

For Company H, 3rd Maine: W. S. Heath, class of 1855, killed in battle; Francis E. Heath, class of 1858.

These companies received their baptism of fire at Bull Run, July 21, 1861, and of the above-named, C. A. Henrickson and Atwood Crosby were taken prisoners there; the latter a voluntary one to care for his brother who was shot through the lungs.*

David Bates was mortally wounded, taken prisoner and died at Richmond, Va., the first Waterville soldier killed; and a number of the Waterville contingent were wounded and captured.

During the year the following changes were made in the line and non-commissioned officers:

Capt. Frank S. Hesseltine, promoted November 14th to major of the 13th Maine.

Lieut. Nath'l Hanscom, promoted November 15th to captain of his company.

2nd Lieut. W. A. Hatch, promoted November 15th to 1st lieutenant of his company.

Capt. W. S. Heath was promoted lieutenant colonel 5th regiment, September 25th.

Lieut. F. E. Heath was promoted captain of his own Company H.

2nd Lieut. Jno. R. Day was promoted 1st lieutenant of his own company.

1st Sergt. E. C. Lowe was promoted 2nd lieutenant of his own company, and

---

*Henrickson was a prisoner eleven months in Libby and Salisbury prisons and the Parish prison in New Orleans; was exchanged and returned to Waterville. In '63 he enlisted in the navy, and was promoted to Ensign. While serving as gunner in the turret of the monitor Saugus, in the second attack on Fort Fisher, one of the 15-inch Rodman guns exploded, prostrating the executive officer and seventeen men in the turret, wounding every man except Henrickson, but, miraculously, killing none.

Sergt. J. H. Plaisted was promoted 1st sergeant of his own company.

These were the changes and casualties of our neighbors and friends at the front for the year 1861, in Companies G and H, 3rd Maine.

Of the boys from our State, 188 were killed or died of disease or wounds, and 165 were prisoners or missing.

The excitement, the ten thousand details of the recruiting, arming, equipping, and transportation of Maine troops to the seat of war; their military discipline there; the campaigns, battles, skirmishes, marches, sickness and deaths among these Maine boys in that first year of the war, filled the minds of the men and women of our town, and of the State, to the almost total exclusion of all else, except sympathy for those who mourned the loss of loved ones, and sympathy for the sick, suffering, homesick, heartsick boys who lingered in the populous hospitals where parting life was laid.

No sooner had our first contingent, Companies G and H, been uniformed at Augusta, than with natural instinct, devotion and helpfulness, the women of Waterville commenced their arduous duties of picking lint, making bandages, seeking contributions of money for hospital stores for soldiers in camp in our State, in the field and general hospitals; and these duties were continuous, untiring, during the war. Commencing in the modest home— individual labor, sympathy and love, developed into the town, county, State and general organizations that spent fabulous sums for the sick and wounded, relieving distress in ways never before known.

The approximate estimate of Waterville's contributions in money, hospital stores, etc., in public channels, from 1861 to 1865 is:

To soldiers in Maine camps and hospitals....	$600 00
To general hospitals in loyal states..........	300 00
To regimental hospitals and individuals......	350 00
To New York, Philadelphia, Boston, etc....	200 00
To United States Sanitary Commission	400 00
To United States Christian Commission	1,500 00
To aid to 652 persons in 215 families........	10,234 42
	$13,584 42

The modest beginnings of individuals and local associations
of relief grew so helpful, so necessary, and finally so vast in
scope, as to eclipse any and all efforts before or since made to
supplement the hospital service of the army in its efforts to alle-
viate suffering. Contributions were enormous. Government
was calling for the last man and the last dollar to *save* the country, and to those at home money seemed worthless *without* country, flag, and honor.

In her "Epistle to Posterity" Mrs. Sherwood says: "Dr. Bellows was president of the Sanitary Commission, and I became
secretary to the Metropolitan Fair and wrote innumerable letters
to all our representatives in Europe. All answered well. After
a winter's work we sent Dr. Bellows *one million three hundred
and sixty-five dollars in one check,* as the result of our work."*

Among the many schemes for the benefit of our soldiers in the
field was a plan for transmitting their pay or a portion of it to
their families at home, authorized by General Orders No. 81,
war department, adjutant general's office, September 19, 1861,
by "Allotment Rolls," to be signed by the soldier who designated
his assignee, his address, and the amount per month to be
reserved. These rolls were transmitted by company and regimental officers to the paymaster general, and by him to the dis-
tributors or trustees appointed by the governor, who generously
and patriotically consented not only to act without compensation,
but to give bonds to Nathan Dane and John S. Hodsdon in the
sum of $15,000 each for the faithful performance of their duties.

The volunteer trustee for Waterville and vicinity was Homer
Percival, Esq., cashier of the Peoples' Bank, who performed the
onerous duties of this office during the war, although many of
these trustees resigned their offices, finding the duties too
exacting.

The amount received and distributed by banks and private
individuals as trustees in these allotment rolls prior to the trans-

---

*The writer has in his possession a fine lithograph receipt of the "Committee
on Military Donations of the City of Boston," reading:

"Boston, 1861"

"This certifies that the ladies of the Waterville Association have given sixty
dollars and thirty cents for the soldiers who leave Boston under the requisition
of the President of the United States."

(signed) Mrs. Harrison Gray Otis
for the Com. on Military Donations.

fer of a part of these duties to the State treasurer by act of the legislature, and the few who continued to discharge those duties without compensation, must amount to some hundreds of thousands of dollars.

The State treasurer alone received and disbursed $559,526.37.

It could only gratify idle curiosity, to indicate how much of this sum came to Waterville from our boys in the field, and in what years, and the suggestion is only made to show how impossible it is to-day to group events chronologically, which most interest us locally. Our neighbors and friends joined this or that regiment and lost their identity in the Grand Army of the Republic, that for four long years held in its grasp, not only the destiny of this Nation, but the fate of Liberty and good government throughout the globe, an army which knew no law but Loyalty, no thought but obedience; an army that served under as many commanders as it fought campaigns; yet marched as cheerfully and fought as loyally under the new commander as under the old; an army that fought over more miles of ground than most continental armies ever marched over; an army baptized in blood, consecrated in tears, and hallowed in prayers.

In such a school, the fathers of this generation, were taught what loyalty meant; what our flag symbolized; while the mothers sat with sorrow and wrought with busy hands and tearful eyes.

From homes of peaceful traditions; lives of peaceful pursuits; our Waterville boys stood up to be counted "for three years or for the war"—anxious to do their duty.

Waterville was represented in each of the fifteen infantry regiments sent out in '61, except the 2nd, 4th, and 12th; as also in the 1st Cavalry and the 4th Battery, as follows:

One in the 1st Infantry; seventy-four in the 3rd Infantry; three in the 5th Infantry; one in the 6th Infantry; eight in the 7th Infantry; fourteen in the 8th Infantry; three in the 9th Infantry; one in the 10th Infantry; two in the 11th Infantry; one in the 13th Infantry; one in the 14th Infantry; one in the 15th Infantry; four in the First Cavalry; one in the 4th Battery.

In 1862 Waterville furnished 102 volunteers for the twelve regiments of infantry and one regiment of heavy artillery, besides recruits, as follows:

Twenty-two for the 16th Infantry; two for the 17th Infantry; eight for the 19th Infantry; twenty-nine for the 20th Infantry; forty-one for the 21st Infantry.

Commissioned officers from Waterville in the 16th: Abner R. Small, Adjutant, promoted Major; William A. Stevens, 2nd Lieut., 1st Lieut., and Captain, killed before Petersburg.

Commissioned officers from Waterville in the 19th: Francis E. Heath, promoted from the 3rd Me., to Lieut.-Col. of the 19th, Colonel and Brevet Brigadier-General; F. W. Haskell, Adjutant.

Commissioned officers from Waterville in the 20th: Isaac S. Bangs, Captain; Lieut.-Col. 81st U. S. C. I.; Col. U. S. colored Heavy Artillery, Brevet Brigadier-General U. S. Vols.; George C. Getchell, 1st Sergt., 2nd Lieut., 1st Lieut., Captain 81st U. S. C. I., Major, Lieut.-Col., and Brevet-Colonel; Addison W. Lewis, 1st Lieut. and Captain; Charles W. Billings, 2nd Lieut., 1st Lieut, and Captain, died of wounds at Gettysburg; Charles R. Shorey, Sergt., 1st Sergt., 2nd Lieut., and 1st Lieut.; W. H. Low, Sergt. and 1st Lieut.; Henry A. Batchelder, Sergt. and 2nd Lieut.

Commissioned officers from Waterville in the 21st Regiment: John U. Hubbard, Captain; George W. Hubbard, Sergt.-Major, 2nd Lieut.; Andrew Pinkham, 2nd Lieut.; Frank Bodfish, Hospital Steward to Asst. Surgeon.

Casualties and Promotions of commissioned officers from Waterville: Lieut.-Colonel W. S. Heath, 5th Me., killed at Gaines Mill; Chaplain Henry C. Leonard, from 3rd to 18th Regt.; William A. Hatch, 1st Lieut. in 3rd Me., and Major 72nd U. S. C. I.; George A. McIntire, 2nd Lieut., 1st Lieut., and Captain; James H. Plaisted, Sergt., Sergt.-Major, to Adjutant and Captain; Samuel Hamblen, to 2nd Lieut., Captain, Major, and Lieut.-Col. in Ullman's Brigade; E. C. Lowe, Sergt., to 2nd Lieut., resigned; Frank H. Getchell, Hospital Steward to Assist. Surgeon; John R. Day, 2nd Lieut. to 1st Lieut. and Captain; Charles W. Lowe, 2nd Lieut. to 1st Lieut. and Captain; William H. Copp, to 1st Lieut. Co. I, 17th Me.; Charles A. Farrington, to Lieut. 31st Me.; Samuel J. Haines, to Lieut. U. S. N.; Henry E. Tozier to Lieut. 8th Me.; John B. Wilson, to Surgeon 96th U. S. C. I.

Waterville furnished for the two regiments of infantry and one of cavalry in 1863: Four for the 29th Infantry; sixteen for the

30th Infantry; two for the 2nd Cavalry; and in 1864: Seventeen for the 31st Infantry; three for the 32nd Infantry; and many recruits for all the regiments and batteries in the field, the unassigned companies, the coast guards and naval service.

The figures given for 1861-2-3-4 being for the regiments, etc., as originally sent to the field, but these and all subsequent allotments of men under the President's call, were always up to the requirements.

In 1861 more than its share was furnished, of men who received no bounty from the government and the town received no credit for the excess.

The enlistments from Waterville for the years 1861 and 1862 can be quite accurately determined, but to ascertain the actual enlistments in any succeeding year, to include recruits, drafted men, and substitutes, is a task of such magnitude that it will never be undertaken, because the results are unimportant and not commensurate with the labor.

The quotas of Waterville and all the other towns and cities for 1863 and subsequent calls were not apportioned to such municipalities, but to the respective provost marshals, districts, sub-districts or to congressional districts, and no adequate record of these apportionments exists.

The foregoing figures show that the enlistments for the original companies in different organizations of named men were 121 in 1861; 102 in 1862; 22 in 1863; and 20 in 1864; while the alphabetical list printed herewith gives the names of 421 men; showing that 156 more men joined these organizations as recruits during these four years, or one in nine of the entire population in 1861.

Waterville paid in bounties for enlistments as follows:

Call of	1861	Nothing	
	1862	3 years men	$4,700
	1862	9 month men	5,200
	1863	Volunteers	8,925
	1864-5	Volunteers and drafted men who furnished substitutes	45,790
		Drafted men that entered service	1,200
		Substitutes	1,900

$67,715

Out of the 400 estimated alumni and undergraduates of Waterville (now Colby) College in 1865, 142 entered service during the war.

Thirty-eight members of Waterville Masonic Lodge entered service and seven were killed in battle.

The State of Maine furnished 72,945 men for the war. The total number of troops killed or died of wounds was 2,801. The total number of troops who died of disease was 4,521. Total. 7,322, or about one in ten of the men who enlisted.

The losses in naval service are not here included.

It is impossible for the present generation to realize the danger, the privation, the suffering of those whom we knew; who went out from among us; or the agonizing suspense of the mothers, wives, sisters and daughters who were left at home; of their waiting, fearing, hoping, as the long campaigns followed each other, leaving in their trail, waste, ruin and lonely graves.

And when battle was on, their faith in God was almost a premonition, while their constant prayer was for hope in his mercy, or strength to bear their pain.

To those who remember the dreadful years of the war, it is no longer real, but a horrid dream of blood, and horror and woe.

These will know that some of our boys followed their tattered flags, representing their State, their town, their home, in every campaign, in every great battle, and every prison of the South.

David Bates, our first martyr, represents Waterville at Bull Run, killed there forty-one years ago this month.

George Bowman and Roscoe Young died at Yorktown.

Lieut.-Col. W. S. Heath, the gallant soldier; so early lost to his home and his country; killed at the disastrous battle of Gaines Mill, where for forty years he has slept under the grass and flowers in an unknown grave.

Miner W. Savage at South Mountain.

Isaac W. Clark at Antietam.

Lorenzo Clark, Charles F. Lyford, James O. West, and John M. Wheeler at Fredericksburg.

William F. Bates, Albert Corson, and Joseph D. Simpson at Gettysburg.

Hadley P. Dyer, Stephen Ellis, and Richard Perley at Port Hudson.

William Chapman, C. R. Atwood, Peter Roderick, and Capt. William A. Stevens before Petersburg.

Lieut. Charles A. Farrington at the Wilderness; commissioned Captain, but died of his wounds in Washington before he could be mustered.

John O. James and Albert Quimby, buried at sea.

Six died at Salisbury prison, two at Andersonville, one at Belle Isle, and one at Camp Gross, Texas.

The yellow fever found a victim in the brilliant young officer, Br. Col. George C. Getchell, at New Orleans, and a soldier's death met our boys at Hatchers Run, Pleasant Hill, La., Weldon Railroad, Chantilly, Ship Island, Winchester, and Belle Plain.

The Bacon family sent five sons; but three returned.

The Messer family sent three sons; none returned.

The "Penney Boys"—four brothers, three killed or died in service, one returned to die at home, of disease contracted in the army.

Deacon Stevens sent his two sons, most promising young men,—both killed in battle.

Companies G and H of the Third Infantry, and Co. A of the 20th Infantry were well known as Waterville companies, and from the first to last, the town furnished eighty-five men for the former, and forty-five for the latter.

Of these, but three are living here of the eighty-five who went to the front in '61, in the Third Regiment,—Charles R. Shorey, F. W. Haskell, and Charles Bacon; in Oakland two, Baxter Crowell and George T. Benson.

Of the forty-five who went into the 20th (Co. A), but two are living in Waterville, I. S. Bangs and Charles R. Shorey, and one in Oakland, William H. Stevens.

Our Roll of Honor contains the names and military record of 140 of our dead, including a few who came here to live at some time since the war and died, and found a resting place in Pine Grove Cemetery. Fifty of these went from here and are buried here. As many more "unheeded—unknown;"—lie where they fell and were thrown into trenches without prayer, or died in hospital and prison and drifted away into the dawning eternities.

Many of these are they who came back to us "when war was done," thro' the blood-red haze of a score of battlefields. These and the living are the representatives of the men who bequeathed to this and the coming generations, in trust forever, the heritage of a Nation saved, which they must learn how to defend.

These are the names of men that in the annals of this fair city deserve imperishable fame, and in reverent spirit let every citizen of Waterville read this

Roll of Honor.

Allen, Benjamin C.: Co. B, 14th Mass. Inf. Vol., afterwards designated as 1st Mass. H'y Art. Died in Amory Square Hospital, Washington, May 23d, 1864, of wounds received at Spottsylvania May 19, 1864.

Aderton, Wm. H.: Private, Co. B, 13th Me.; died July 17, 1862, of disease, at Ship Island.

Atwood, Charles R.: Sergeant, Co. B, 32nd Me.; killed, July 30th, 1864, at Petersburg.

Balentine, Elijah: Private, Co. L, 4th Mass. Cav. Buried here.

Balentine, Samuel: Corporal, Co. K, 7th Me. Vols. Died December 29, 1883. Buried here.

Bates, David: Private, Co. G, 3d Me. Killed at Bull Run, July 21, 1861. First man killed from Waterville.

Bowman, Geo. W., Jr.: Private, Co. E, 3rd Me. Died at Yorktown, May 13, 1862.

Brackett, Orrin: Private, 6th Me. Battery. Died at Waterville, March 21, 1863.

Bickford, Bennett: Private, Co. E, 30th Me. Died at New Orleans, May 4, 1864.

Bacon, Chas.: Private, Co. G, 3rd Me. Died at City Point, 1864.

Boothby, Warren J.: Private, Co. I, 31st Me. Died at Waterville, April 24, 1869.

Blair, John: Private, Co. B, 16th Me., Co. G, 20th Me. Died at Fairfield, 1891.

Bacon, Wm. H.: Corporal, 3rd Me. Died at Waterville, 1862.

Barrett, Wm. K.: Private, Co. H, 3rd Me. Died at Libby Prison or Belle Isle. Date unknown.

Bates, Isaac W.: Private, Co. F, 32nd Me. Died at Salisbury Prison.

Bates, Wm. T.: Private, Co. E, 16th Me. Killed at Battle of Gettysburg, July 2, 1863.

Bates, Phineas: Private, Co. F, 32nd Me. Died in Salisbury Prison.

Blake, Geo. E. A.: Private. Co. E, 8th Me. Killed at Hatcher's Run, Va., April 2, 1865.

Butler, Daniel: Private, Co. B, 12th Me. Inf. Vet. Vol. Died here, June 18, 1896.

Bushey, Levi: Co. I, 8th Me. Died December 15, 1900.

Bushey, William: Private, Co. C, 9th Maine. Died here, June 15, 1902. Buried here.

Levi Cayouette: Private, Co. E., 30th Me. Died here, August 19, 1902. Buried here.

Copp, Wm. H.: 1st Lieut., Co. I, 17th Me. Died in Minnesota, April, 1883.

Copp, Alonzo: Private, Co. B, 34th Regt. Pa. Vol. and 5th Pa. Reserves; private, Co. C, 191st Pa. Died in Salisbury Prison, of starvation, December 28, 1864.

Cary, Joseph: Private, Co. A, 7th Me. Died in Waterville. Buried here.

Crosby, Atwood: Asst. Surgeon, U. S. Navy, Co. G, 3rd Me. Died in Las Vegas, N. M., January 25, 1883. Buried here.

Chapman, William: Private, Co. D, 8th Me.; Co. E, 27th Me. Killed at Petersburg, June 15, 1864.

Clark, Lorenzo D.: Private, Co. A, 20th Me. Died at Fredericksburg, Va., 1863.

Clark, Isaac W.: Private, Co. A, 20th Me. Died at Antietam, November, 1862.

Clark, Charles: Co. I, 3rd Me. Regt. Transferred to 3rd U. S. Artillery.

Cochran, Hiram: Private, Co. K. 3rd Me. Wounded at Gettysburg, July 3rd, 1863. Died in Libby Prison, December 23rd, 1863.

Cochran, Thaddeus: Private, Co. C, 41st Mass. Died at Alexandria, La., in hospital.

Corson, Albert: Co. H, 3rd Regt. Died of wounds, July 2, 1863.

Dusty, Frank: Private, Co. I, 31st Me. Died here, of wounds, April 10, 1866. Buried here.

De Wolfe, Wm. H.: Private, Co. M, 1st Me. Heavy Art. Died at Washington, of wounds, June 11, 1864. Buried here.

Davis, Octavius A.: Private Co. K, 1st D. C. Cav. Died in Salisbury prison, November 4, 1864.

Dyer, Hadley P.: Sergeant Co. B, 21st Me. Died at Cairo, Ill., en route home, of wounds received at Port Hudson.

Dubor, Isaac: Private, Co. A, Me. Coast Guards. Died here, April 15, 1869.

Davis, Arba P.: Corporal, Co. I, 31st Me. Died here, November 30, 1885.

Ellis, Stephen: Private, Co. B, 21st Me. Killed at Port Hudson, May 27, 1863.

Euarde, Paulette: Private, Co. A, 9th Me. Died of wounds, July 24, 1864.

Ellis, Dighton: Co. E, 1st Regt. Veteran Infantry.

Folsom, Samuel P.: Private, 3rd Me. Died December 22, 1861.

Farrington, Charles A.: Lieut. 31st Me. Died at Washington, June 20, 1864, of wounds received at the Battle of the Wilderness.

Farnham, Wm. H.: Private, Co. B, 21st Me. Died at New Orleans, May 16, 1863.

Fish, Hiram: Co. H, 3rd Regt. Died at Hospital, Harrison's Landing.

Getchell, Geo. C.: Bvt. Lieut.-Col. U. S. Vols.; Major, 81st U. S. C. I. Died of yellow fever at New Orleans, September 21, 1866. Buried here.

Gibbs, Thos. A.: Private, Co. G, 16th Me. Died Dec. 9, 1863. Body brought home. Buried here.

Gibbs, David B., Jr.: Private, Co. B, 14th Me. Died, April 1, 1863.

Gilcot, Frank: Private, Co. I, 31st Me. No headstone; no record.

Grant, Isaiah: Private, Co. F, 32nd Me. Died here, December 22, 1882. Buried here.

Hardy, D. W.: Assistant Surgeon, Surgeon, U. S. Col'd Inf. Died at Billerica, Mass., July 28, 1901. Buried here.

Herbert, Edw. B.: Private, 1st Me. Cav. Died at Washington, D. C., of wounds, May 3, 1865. Returned prisoner.

Hubbard, Albro: Sergeant, Co. H, 3rd Me. Released from Andersonville, March 10. Died at Annapolis, Md., March 16, 1864, from effects of want and exposure at Andersonville.

Heath, W. S.: Lieut.-Col. 5th Me. Killed at Gaines Mill, June 27, 1862.

Ham, W. H.: Private, 31st Me. Died at Poplar Grove Church, Va., November 26, 1864.

Hayward, W. E.: Co. A, 1st Mass. Died here, August 19, 1869. Buried here.

Haynes, Samuel J.: Lieut., U. S. Navy. Died here, May, 1892. Buried here.

Heath, Francis Edw.: Col., 19th Me. Brevet Brig. General. Died here, December 20, 1897.

Herrick, Algernon P.: Co. G, 3rd Regt. Taken Prisoner, July 2, 1863. Died in prison.

Hubbard, A. J.: Capt. Co. F, 31st Me. Died at Morganza, La., July 16, 1864. Capt. Hubbard was twin brother of Capt. Geo. W. and brother of Capt. John U.; was born in Waterville, lived here until past his majority and went into the service from the west.

Jero, Joseph: Private, 30th Me. Died in prison at Camp Gross, Texas, December 1, 1864.

James, John O.: Seaman, ship "Colorado." Died at sea of yellow fever, September 10, 1863.

Jackson, John: Private, 1st Me. Heavy Art. Died here, April 3, 1875. Buried here.

Keith, Sidney: Private, Co. A, 20th Me. Died, October 10, 1890. Buried here.

King, Moses: Private, 30th Me. Died on steamer near Portland, August 26, 1865, when returning home.

Kelley, Moses: Chaplain Soldiers Home, Togus; Chaplain U. S. Army from 1870 to 1879, when he was retired. Died at Damariscotta, Me., August 25, 1898. Buried here.

Lowe, Chas. W.: Captain, Co. G, 3rd Me. Died at Skowhegan, April 11, 1887. Buried there.

Lyford, Chas. F.: Private, 16th Me. Killed at Fredericksburg, Va., December 14, 1862.

Libby, B. M.: Private, Co. I, 31st Me. Buried here.

La Fontaine, Alex: Private, Co. H, 7th Me. Died, March 26, 1886. Buried here.

Loring, E. P.: Lieut.-Col. 10th U. S. Heavy Art. Col. Died in Boston, October 30, 1894. Buried here.

Messer, Orin: Private, Co. E, 7th Me. Taken prisoner at Spottsylvania, May 12, 1864. Died in Libby prison, of wounds.

Messer, Alvin: Private, Co. G, 7th Me. Died at Alexandria, September 24, 1862.

Messer, John N.: Private, Co. G, 7th Me. Killed on skirmish line, May 12, 1864, at Spottsylvania, Va.

Macomber, Otis: Private, Co. K, 16th Me. Died at Belle Plain, Va., March 15, 1863. Buried here.

Murray, Lewis: Private, Co. B, 16th Me. Killed at Fredericksburg, December 13th, 1862.

McFarland, Ira I.: 1st Me. Cav. Died at Waterville, February 8, 1864. Buried here.

Marston, Wm. H.: Sergeant, 32nd Mass. Died at Winchester, Va., in hospital. Date unknown.

Paine, John A.: 5th Me. Battery. Died at Portland, May 20, 1871. Buried here.

Penney, Jos. M.: Sergeant, Co. B, 7th Me. Died here, November 19, 1862. Was at home on furlough when he died. Buried here.

Penney, Wm. W.: Private, 15th Me. Died at New Orleans, March 5, 1864. Buried here.

Penney, Peletiah: Private, 3rd Me. Died at Washington, November 1, 1862. Buried here.

Penney, Ira D.: Private, 31st Me. Died at Salisbury prison, January 10, 1865, of starvation and despair; died "crying for bread."

Percival, Albert W.: Private, Engineer Corps. Died here, August 23, 1872. Buried here.

Percival, Wm. C.: Seaman, U. S. Navy. Killed at Bangor in railroad accident, August 9, 1871.

Percival, Geo. G.: Assistant Surgeon, 80th U. S. C. I. Died here, August 3, 1882. Buried here.

Pease, Elias: Private, Co. K., 14th Me. Buried here.

Perley, Richard: Private, 21st Me. Killed at Port Hudson, May 27, 1863.

Perry, Joseph: Private, 3rd Me. Wounded and made prisoner at Chantilly, August 31, 1862, and never heard from.

Perry, James: Private, Co. G, 3rd Me. Died here, April 15, 1875. Buried here.

Peters, Thomas: Private, Co. H, 12th Me. Died here, March 7, 1902.

Phelps, Lewis G.: Private, Co. G, 16th Me. Died July 28, 1863. Buried here.

Phelps, Wm. H.: Private, Co. H, 13th Me.; Co. H, 30th Me.

Plummer, Edwin: Private, Co. B, 21st Me. Died at Port Hudson, La., July 24, 1863.

Pooler, Peter: Co. C, 28th Mass. Inf. Buried here.

Pooler, Jos.: Private, 1st Me., Heavy Art. Died at Portsmouth, July 14, 1864, of wounds.

Pooler, Ephraim: Private, Co. E, 30th Me. Died at Waterville, October 15, 1868. Buried here.

Pooler, Henry: Private, Co. H, 30th Me. Died at New Orleans, July 11, 1864.

Pooler, Jos.: Private, Co. E, 19th Me. Died here, January 23, 1887. Buried here.

Prescott, E. E.: 21st Me. Died here, April 18, 1874. Buried here.

Proctor, Sumner B.: Private, Co. F, Me. Coast Guards. Died here, July 16, 1892. Buried here.

Pullen, James Burney: Corporal, Co. E, 30th Me. Wounded at Pleasant Hill, La. Died in prison, April 29, 1864.

Quimby, Albert: Private, 30th Me. Died on steamer en route to New Orleans and buried at sea, March 17, 1864.

Ricker, James F.: Private, Co. G, 3rd Me. Died at Alexandria, Va., Sept. 11, 1861.

Rodrick, Peter: Private, 19th Me. Killed on picket before Petersburg, November 12, 1864.

Rice, Thos. G.: Lieutenant, 2nd Me. Cav. Buried here.

Roberts, Winslow: Lieutenant, Co. I, 14th Me.; Captain, Co. H, 14th Me.; Captain, Co. G, Maine Coast Guards. Died here, June 17, 1879. Buried here.

Ronco, Jos.: Private, Co. K, 29th Me. Died in Waterville. Buried here.

Richards, Jos.: Private, Co. B, 21st Me. Died here, March 3, 1892. Buried here in Catholic cemetery.

Ronco, Abram, 2nd: Private, Co. A, 9th Me. Died here, Sepember 10, 1891. Buried here.

Richardson, Royal: Private, Co. B, 21st Me. Died here, September 20, 1863.

Roderick, John: Private, Co. A, 20th Me. Died here, November 17, 1898. Buried here.

Savage, Miner W.: Corporal, 12th Mass. Killed at South Mountain, September 17, 1862.

Simpson, Jos. D.: Corporal, Co. A, 20th Me. Killed at Gettysburg, July 2, 1863.

Shepherd, Rich A.: Private, Co. C, 19th Me. Killed in the battle of the Wilderness, May 7, 1864.

Stevens, Wm. A.: Captain 16th Me. Killed near Petersburg, June 19, 1864. Buried here.

Stevens, Edwin C.: Sergeant Major, 16th Me. Killed at the Weldon Railroad, August 18, 1864. Buried here.

Sawtelle, John R.: 3rd Me. Died August 18, 1862. Buried here.

Scates, Edgar: Private, Co. A, 20th Me. Died at Portland, March 29, 1881. Buried here.

Soule, Daniel A.: Private, Co. E, 16th Me. Died here, October 13, 1883. Buried here.

Stevens, Jason R.: Private, Co. D, 7th Me. Died in Waterville, 1863. Buried here.

Stevens, G. G.: 26th Co. Unassigned.

Saunders, Theodore O.: 1st Sergeant, Co. G, 62nd Ill. Died at Soldiers' Home at Togus, July 3, 1896. Buried here.

Tilley, George M.: Private, Co. I, 31st Me. Died at Augusta, Me., April 2, 1864.

Thayer, Adin B.: Private, Co. B, 16th Me. Taken prisoner at Weldon Railroad, August 18, 1864. Died at Salisbury prison.

Tallouse, Martin: Private, 16th Me. Wounded and missing at battle of Weldon Railroad, October 18, 1864.

Tozier, Henry E.: Captain, Co. I, 8th Me. Killed at Fort Holly, Spring Hill, Va., December 10, 1864. Buried there.

Tozier, Albert F.: Private, Co. H, 11th Me. Died at Waterville, March 13, 1865. Buried here.

Tozier, W. M.: Private, Co. E, 30th Me. Died at Pleasant Hill, La., of wounds, December 1, 1864. Buried here.

West, Wallace W.: Hospital Lieutenant, 8th Me. Died here, February 5, 1862.

Wyman, Wm. W.: Sergeant, 3rd and 21st Me. Died of wounds received at Port Hudson, June 1, 1863.

Woodman, Erastus D.: Corporal, 14th U. S. I. Died at Washington under surgeon's hands while undergoing amputation of his leg.

Wheeler, George L.: Private, Co. G, 3rd Me. Killed at Chantilly, September 1, 1862.

West, James O.: Private, 31st Me. Died at Fredericksburg, May 23, 1864, of wounds.

Wilson, John B.: Surgeon, 96th U. S. C. I. Died at Dexter, March 15, 1866. Buried here.

Washburn, John N.: No record.

Wheeler, John M.: Private, Co. G, 16th Me. Wounded at Fredericksburg, December 13. Died December 18, 1862.

White, Henry: 2nd Battery, 1st Mounted Artillery; 1st Cavalry.

Young, Eben W: Private, 3rd Me. Died in prison at Columbus, Ga., March 26, 1864.

Young, Eugene H.: Co. H, 3rd Me. Died here, February 19, 1893.

Young, Roscoe G: Private, Co. H, 3rd Me. Died at Yorktown, Va., April 22, 1862.

> "The long years come and go,
> And the Past,
> The sorrowful, splendid Past,
> With its glory and its woe,
> Seems never to have been.
>
> *   *   *   *   *   *
>
> Seems never to have been?
> O sombre days and grand,
> How ye crowd back again,
> Seeing our heroes' graves are green.
>
> *   *   *   *   *   *

> Tears will well to our eyes,
> And the bitter doubt will rise—
> But hush! for the strife is done,
> Forgiven are wound and scar;
> The fight was fought and won
> Long since, on sea and shore,
> And every scattered star
> Set in the blue once more;
> We are one as before,
> With the blot from our scutcheon gone!"

The writer began more than four years ago, the preparation of a list of the soldiers who served in the Civil War from the town of Waterville; intending to print the same for distribution among our citizens.

It has been a fascinating pursuit, a labor of love; better, a tribute to the living and the dead of our brave volunteers.

In pursuit of detailed information in regard to the military record of different soldiers, inquiry developed interesting statistics in regard to previous wars in which this country has been engaged and in which citizens of Waterville bore a part. These have accumulated until they cover something of the details of the Revolutionary War, the War of 1812, the Aroostook War, the Mexican War, the War of the Rebellion, the War with Spain and the Phillippine War. All too long, the preservation of precious material has been delayed. What has been secured the writer hopes will prove of interest if printed here.

Sixty years ago, more than a score of Revolutionary soldiers lived here, who carried all the material in their memory, for a record of their lives.

Fifty years ago the War of 1812 could have been intelligently rehearsed by men living. The same is true of the Mexican. The facts, so important historically and so difficult of proof to-day, were rehearsed for years by men whose memory was better than books.

Survivors of the Civil War, who went from Waterville, are scattered far and wide over the length and breadth of this country and will never return.

The feeling of the writer has been, that it was a duty someone owed to the boys of '61; the least of whom, from here, took his life in his hand with his rifle, and living or dead deserves a record.

The simple alphabetical list indicates little of the labor required to perfect it, or the great expense of research, copying and recopying, typewriting and material. It is not claimed to-day as perfect, but perfection has been aimed at, and if any one who is interested can discover an error, the writer will be grateful for information.

The list contains the name of every soldier who enlisted from Waterville, or who, having been born and reared here, left home, and when war was declared enlisted in another town or state.

The writer trusts the citizens of Waterville will appreciate the list and the labor.

Grateful acknowledgments are tendered to the very able and soldierly Adjutant-General John T. Richards, and his chief clerk, Thomas Clark, for valuable information and careful revision of the list, as well as to the courteous Colonel F. C. Ainsworth, chief, Record and Pension office of the war department, for valuable advice and prompt and painstaking replies to all inquiries.

Much kindness has also been shown the writer by Hon. Wm. M. Olin, secretary of the Commonwealth of Massachusetts, to whom thanks are due for Civil War and Revolutionary records.

WATERVILLE SOLDIERS IN THE WAR OF THE REBELLION.

Aderton, Wm. H., 13th Infantry, volunteer; Alexander, Geo. E., 1st cavalry, volunteer; Allen, Manley, 19th Infantry, substitute; Allen, Benjamin C., 14th Massachusetts, volunteer; Atkinson, Leroy, 7th Infantry, volunteer; Atwood, Chas. R., 32nd Infantry, volunteer; Avery, John, 21st Infantry, volunteer.

Bacon, Chas., 3rd Infantry, volunteer; Bacon, John H., 3rd Infantry, volunteer; Bacon, W. H., 3rd Infantry, volunteer; Bacon, James R., 7th Infantry, volunteer; Bacon, George, 7th Infantry, volunteer; Bagley, Alexander, 19th Infantry, substitute; Balentine, William, 16th Infantry, volunteer; Balentine, Elijah, 4th Massachusetts, volunteer; Bangs, I. S., 20th Infantry, volunteer; Barney, Henry, 3rd Infantry, volunteer; Barrett, Wm. K., 3rd Infantry, volunteer; Bartlett, Nelson G., Coast Guards, volunteer; Basford, Andrew J., 19th Infantry, drafted; Bates, David, 3rd Infantry, volunteer; Bates, Geo. W., U. S. Navy, volunteer; Bates, John H., 20th Infantry, volunteer; Bates, Wm.

F., 16th Infantry, volunteer; Benson, Geo. F., 3rd Infantry, volunteer; Bickford, Levi S., 3rd Infantry, volunteer; Bickford, Bennett, 30th Infantry, volunteer; Bickford, Cyrus, 20th Infantry, volunteer; Billings, Hiram, 15th Infantry, volunteer; Black, Portal M., 7th Infantry, volunteer; Blackstone, Daniel, 8th Infantry, volunteer; Blackstone, Daniel, 31st Infantry, volunteer; Blackstone, Chas. H., 32nd Infantry, volunteer; Blackstone, Geo. C., 32nd Infantry, volunteer; Blackwell, Sam'l H., 52nd Massachusetts, volunteer; Blair, John, 16th Infantry, substitute; Blake, Geo. A. E., 8th Infantry, volunteer; Bodfish, Frank, 21st Infantry, volunteer; Boothby, Warren, 31st Infantry, volunteer; Bow, Horace, 3rd Infantry, volunteer; Bowden, Henry H., 21st Infantry, volunteer; Bowlett, Frederic, 21st Infantry, volunteer; Bowman, Geo. W., 3rd Infantry, volunteer; Brackett, Orrin, 6th Battery, volunteer; Branch, Milton M., 1st D. C. Cavalry and 1st Cavalry, volunteer; Branch, Chas. H., U. S. Navy, substitute; Branch, Elisha R., U. S. Navy, substitute; Bray, Robert, ——— substitute; Brooks, Wm. E., 16th Infantry, volunteer; Brown, James, 1st Cavalry, volunteer; Brown, Wm. W., 15th Infantry, volunteer; Bryant, Geo. H., Coast Guards, volunteer; Bubier, John, 20th Infantry, substitute; Burns, John W., 19th Infantry, substitute; Bushey, Levi, 8th Infantry, volunteer; Bussford, Andrew J., 19th Infantry, drafted; Butler, Thomas, 8th Infantry, volunteer; Bowman, M. T. V., 1st Cavalry, volunteer.

Calder, John G., 1st Veteran Infantry, substitute; Campbell, Augustus, 19th Infantry, substitute; Carey, Joseph, 7th Infantry, volunteer; Carson, Chas. J., 1st Cavalry, volunteer; Cayouette, Levi, 30th Infantry, volunteer; Chandler, Henry A., 16th Infantry, substitute; Chapman, Wm., 8th Infantry, volunteer; Chase, George, 19th Infantry, substitute; Chick, Isaac, 15th Infantry, volunteer; Clark, Albert M., 20th Infantry, volunteer; Clark, Charles, 3rd Infantry, volunteer; Clark, Isaac W., 20th Infantry, volunteer; Clark, Lorenzo D., 20th Infantry, volunteer; Clifford, Selden I., 21st Infantry, volunteer; Clukey, Chas. H., 13th Infantry, volunteer; Cochran, Robert, 3rd Infantry, volunteer; Cochran, Andrew, 31st Infantry, volunteer; Cochran, Hiram, 3rd Infantry, volunteer; Cook, Moses W., 16th Infantry, volunteer; Copp, Alonzo, 5th Pennsylvania Reserves and 19th Regiment

WATERVILLE IN THE WAR.   27

Pennsylvania Volunteers, volunteer; Copp, Wm. H., 3rd Infantry, volunteer; Corson, Albert, 3rd Infantry, volunteer; Cousens, Prentiss M., 12th Infantry, volunteer; Cross, Chas. E., 16th Infantry, volunteer; Cross, Carlostine, 17th Infantry, substitute; Cross, Joseph, 16th Infantry, substitute; Crowell, Henry, 3rd Infantry, volunteer; Crowell, Baxter, 3rd Infantry, volunteer; Cummings, Walter L., 15th Infantry, volunteer; Cunningham, Francis M., 15th Infantry, volunteer; Curtis, James M., 3rd Infantry, volunteer; Cushman, Andrew J., 8th Infantry, volunteer.

Davis, Arba P., 31st Infantry, volunteer; Davis, Daniel B., 9th Infantry, volunteer; Davis, Geo. W., 3rd Infantry, volunteer; Davis, Octavus A., D. C. Cavalry, volunteer; Day, John R., 3rd Infantry, volunteer; Day, Isaac C., 20th Infantry, volunteer; Dearborn, Geo. H., 19th Infantry, volunteer; Deleware, Geo., 30th Infantry, volunteer; Derocher, Chas. W., 3rd Infantry, volunteer; Derocher, Henry, 3rd Infantry, volunteer; DeWolf, Wm. H., 1st Heavy Artillery, volunteer; Dore, Henry A., 19th Infantry, substitute; Dow, Levi A., 21st Infantry, volunteer; Downes, Geo. A., 19th Infantry, substitute; Drake, Nelson, V. S.; Dusty, Frank, 31st Infantry, volunteer; Dusty, James, 8th Infantry, volunteer; Dyer, Hadley P., 3rd and 21st Infantry, volunteer; Dyer, James A., U. S. Navy, substitute.

Eames, Luther N., 3rd Infantry, volunteer; Ellis, Luther, 6th Battery, volunteer; Ellis, Stephen, 21st Infantry, volunteer; Ellis, Sullivan, 21st Infantry, volunteer; Ellis, Dighton, 1st Maine Veteran Infantry, volunteer; Emery, Fanuel H., 20th Infantry, volunteer; Emery, John W., 26th Massachusetts, volunteer; Emery, Nath'l S., D. C. Cavalry, volunteer; Emery, Samuel D., 14th Massachusetts, volunteer; Enman, Paul, 30th Infantry, volunteer; Euarde, Paulette, 9th Infantry, volunteer; Evans, Leander H., 8th Infantry, substitute.

Fairbanks, Henry L., 3rd Infantry, volunteer; Fairbanks, Henry N., 3rd Infantry, volunteer; Farrington, Chas. A., 31st Infantry, volunteer; Fenno, Chas. A., 3rd Infantry, volunteer; Fish, Hiram, 3rd Infantry, volunteer; Folsom, Samuel P., 1st Infantry, volunteer; Foster, Dennis M., 20th Infantry, volunteer; Frazier, Dudley C., 1st Heavy Artillery, volunteer; Frizzle, Geo.

B., Coast Guards, volunteer; Frost, Henry M., 7h Infantry, volunteer; Fuller, Franklin Z., U. S. Navy, substitute.

Galusha, Cyrus C., 13th Infantry, volunteer; Garland, John, Jr., 21st Infantry, volunteer; Garney, George, 1st Cavalry, volunteer; Gayrough, George, 7th Infantry, volunteer; Gerald, Ezekiel, 20th Infantry, volunteer; Gerough, Joseph, 30th Infantry, volunteer; Getchell, Frank H., 3rd Infantry, volunteer; Getchell, Geo. C., 20th Infantry, volunteer; Getchell, Marshall P., 9th Infantry, volunteer; Gibbs, John F., 31st Infantry and 16th Massachusetts, volunteer; Gibbs, Thomas A., 16th Infantry, volunteer; Gibbs, David B., 14th Infantry, volunteer; Gibbs, David B., Jr., 14th Infantry, volunteer; Gibbs, John F., 16th Massachusetts, volunteer; Gilbear, Chas., 7th Infantry, volunteer; Gilcott, Frank, 31st Infantry, volunteer; Gleason, Russell, 21st Infantry, volunteer; Gleason, Geo. R., 21st Infantry, volunteer; Goff, Alonzo, 21st Infantry, volunteer; Goff, Alonzo, 31st Infantry, volunteer; Gonnea, Geo., 9th Infantry, volunteer; Goodrich, Daniel, drafted; Goodridge, Foster, 1st Veteran Infantry, volunteer; Goodwin, John F., 3rd Infantry, volunteer; Gordon, Edmund, 2nd Infantry, volunteer; Goulding, Henry, 3rd Infantry, volunteer; Gray, Albert J., 19th Infantry, substitute; Gullifer, Moses H., D. C. Cavalry, volunteer.

Haines, Samuel J., Lieutenant U. S. Navy, volunteer; Ham, Wm. H., 31st Infantry, volunteer; Hamblen, Samuel, 3rd Infantry, volunteer; Hanuth, John H., V. S., volunteer; Haskell, Frank W., 3rd Infantry, volunteer; Hatch, Frederick C., D. C. Cavalry, volunteer; Hatch, Joseph H., 20th Infantry, volunteer; Hatch, Wm. A., 3rd Infantry, volunteer; Hawes, Wilson, 19th Infantry, substitute; Heath, Wm. S., 3rd Infantry, volunteer; Heath, Francis E., 3rd Infantry, volunteer; Henrickson, Chas. A., 3rd Infantry, volunteer; Herbert, Edward B., 1st Maine Cavalry, volunteer; Herbert, Thos. G., U. S. Navy, substitute; Herrick, Algernon P., 3rd Infantry, volunteer; Hersom, Milford, 3rd Infantry, volunteer; Hersom, Samuel T., 21st Infantry, volunteer; Hersom, Wm. H., 21st Infantry, volunteer; Hesseltine, Frank S., 3rd Infantry, volunteer; Higgins, Albert H., 1st Cavalry, volunteer; Hill, George, substitute; Hitchings, Frank E., 16th Infantry, volunteer; Hodgdon, John S., 11th Infantry, volunteer; Horn, Hiram, 17th Infantry, drafted; Horn, Llewellyn, 15th Infantry, volunteer; Houghton, Daniel F., 16th Infantry, volunteer; Howes, Wilson, 19th Infantry, volunteer; Huard, Paul, 9th Infantry, volunteer; Hubbard, Albro, 3rd Infantry, volunteer; Hubbard, Geo. W., 21st Infantry, volunteer; Hubbard, John W., 21st Infantry, volunteer; Hutchins, Parker P., 20th Infantry, volunteer.

James, Isaiah H., 3rd Infantry, volunteer; James, John, O., U. S. Navy, volunteer; Jibbear, Chas., 7th Infantry, volunteer; Jones, Geo. J., 21st Infantry, volunteer; Joy, Wm. P., 19th Infantry, volunteer.

Keene, Josiah T., 11th Infantry, volunteer; Keith, Sidney, 20th Infantry, volunteer; Kendall, Chas., 14th Infantry, volunteer; King, Moses, 21st Infantry, volunteer; King, John, 20th Infantry, volunteer; Kirby, John J., volunteer; Knox, Sylvester, 3rd Infantry, volunteer; Knox, William, 15th Infantry, volunteer; Knox, Sylvanus, 19th Infantry, volunteer.

Lachanse, Veidal, 16th Infantry, volunteer; Lashus, Geo., 3rd Infantry, volunteer; Latlip, Gott, 29th Infantry, volunteer; Latlip, Geo., 7th Infantry, volunteer; Leonard, Henry C., 3rd Infantry (chaplain), volunteer; Lewis, Solomon B., 3rd Infantry, volunteer; Lewis, David J., 20th Infantry, volunteer; Lewis, Addison W., 20th Infantry, volunteer; Libby, Henry H., substitute; Libby, Albert L., 6th Infantry, volunteer; Littlefield, Geo., 3rd Infantry, volunteer; Lonelon, Chas. W., V. S.; Lore, Wm., 16th Infantry, substitute; Love, Chas., 20th Infantry, volunteer; Lowe, Edw. C., 13th Infantry, volunteer; Lowe, Edw. C., 3rd Infantry, volunteer; Lowe, Chas. W., 3rd Infantry, volunteer; Lowe, Wm. H., 20th Infantry, volunteer; Lowe, Franklin B., D. C. Cavalry, volunteer; Lowell, A. M., U. S. Navy, substitute; Lubier, Gott, 8th Infantry, volunteer; Lyford, Chas. F., 16th Infantry, volunteer; Lyford, James M., 16th Infantry, volunteer.

Maines, Geo., Jr., U. S. Navy, substitute; Mains, Graham, U. S. A., volunteer; Manton, Wm. H., 32nd Massachusetts, volunteer; Marshall, Joseph, 30th Infantry, volunteer; Marston, Watson, 3rd Infantry, volunteer; Martin, Daniel E., 15th Infantry, volunteer; Mason, Fred T., 11th Infantry, volunteer; Maury, Joseph, 16th Infantry, volunteer; Maxham, Geo. M., 5th Infantry, volunteer; Merchant, Harrison, 16th Infantry, volunteer; Merrill, Chas. W., Hancock's Corps, volunteer; Merton, Ernest, 19th Infantry, substitute; Messer, John N., 7th Infantry, volunteer; Messer, Orrin, 7th Infantry, volunteer; Messer, Alvin, 7th Infantry, volunteer; Messer, Eugene P., 30th Infantry, volunteer; McCartney, Wm. H., 21st Infantry, volunteer; McDonald, Hugh, Sharpshooters, volunteer; McDonald, Dugald, 31st Infantry, volunteer; McFadden, Michael, 3rd Infantry, volunteer; McGilvery, John, 16th Infantry, volunteer; McGrath, Daniel, 29th Infantry, volunteer; McIntire, Geo. A., 3rd Infantry, volunteer; McLaughlin, Timothy, 20th Infantry, volunteer; Morrison, John, 19th Infantry, substitute; Mosher, Francis B., 21st Infantry, volunteer; Mosher, Madison, 21st Infantry, volunteer; Morton, Wm. H., 32nd Massachusetts, volunteer; Murphy, Chas. D., V. S.; Murray, Louis, 16th Infantry, volunteer; Muzzey, Geo. E., 20th Infantry, volunteer; Muzzey, Geo. E., 7th Infantry, drafted.

Newland, Wm. H., 21st Infantry, volunteer; Nickerson, Hezekiah, 1st Cavalry, volunteer; Nock, Sylvanus, 6th Battery, volunteer; Noyes, Alonzo, 5th Infantry, volunteer.

Oliver, Frank H., 15th Infantry, volunteer; Oliver, Fayette, 3rd Infantry, volunteer.

Paige, Ezekiel, Jr., 14th Infantry, volunteer; Parker, John H., 11th Infantry, substitute; Parker, Benj., 3rd Infantry, volunteer; Pattee, Orlando J., 21st Infantry, volunteer; Pattee, Orlando I., Coast Guards, volunteer; Peasley, Richard, 21st Infantry, volunteer; Peavey, John M., 9th Infantry, volunteer; Peavy, Wm. D., 3rd Infantry, volunteer; Penney, Chas. H., 21st Infantry, volunteer; Penney, Ira D., 31st Infantry, volunteer; Penney, Everett A., 19th Infantry, volunteer; Penney, Wm. W., 15th Infantry, volunteer; Penney, Peltiah, 3rd Infantry, volunteer; Penney, Joseph M., 7th Infantry, volunteer; Percival, Edw. S., 3rd Infantry, volunteer; Percival, Albert W., U. S. A., volunteer; Percival, Henry H., U. S. A., volunteer Percival, Geo. G., 80th U. S. C. I., volunteer; Perkins, James L., 21st Infantry, volunteer; Perley, Richard, 21st Infantry, volunteer; Perley, Nathaniel, 3rd Infantry, volunteer; Perley, Henry J., 3rd Infantry, volunteer; Perry, George, 8th Infantry, volunteer; Perry, Chas., 8th Infantry, volunteer; Perry, James, 3rd Infantry, volunteer; Perry, Joseph, 3rd Infantry, volunteer; Perry, David, 7th Infantry, volunteer; Phelps, Wm. H., 13th Infantry, volunteer; Pinkham, Andrew, 21st Infantry, volunteer; Plaisted, James H., 3rd Infantry, volunteer; Plummer, Edwin, 21st Infantry, volunteer; Plummer, John H., 6th Battery, volunteer; Pooler, Henry, 30th Infantry, volunteer; Pooler, Gott, 7th Infantry, volunteer; Pooler, Ephriam, 30th Infantry, volunteer; Pooler, Joseph, 1st Heavy Artillery, volunteer; Pooler, Joseph, 16th Infantry, volunteer; Pooler, George, 29th Infantry, volunteer; Porter, John, 9th Infantry, volunteer; Porter, Andrew H., 6th Battery, volunteer; Preo, Peter, 8th Infantry, volunteer; Prescott, Edmund E., 21st Infantry, volunteer; Preson, Thos. E., Hancock's Corps, volunteer; Pulsifer, Alexander W., 16th Infantry, volunteer; Pullen, Frank D., 3rd Infantry, volunteer; Pullen, James Burney, 30th Infantry, volunteer.

Quimby, Clement, 5th Infantry, volunteer; Quimby, Albert, 30th Infantry, volunteer.

Ranco, Moses, 8th Infantry, volunteer; Ranco, Abram, 9th Infantry, volunteer; Ranco, George, 31st Infantry, volunteer; Ranco, Joseph, 10th Infantry, volunteer; Rankins, Lucius, 8th Infantry, volunteer; Rankins, William, 20th Infantry, volunteer; Ray, Robert, U. S. Navy, substitute; Richards, Joseph, 21st Infantry, volunteer; Ricker, James F., 3rd Infantry, volunteer; Roderick, John, 20th Infantry, volunteer; Roderick, Peter, 19th Infantry, volunteer; Rodgers, Edwin J., substitute; Ronco, Frank, 29th Infantry, volunteer; Rowan, David, V. |S.; Rowe, Elisha M., 3rd Infantry, volunteer; Rowe, Welcome, 3rd Infantry, volunteer; Rowe, Addison H., 9th Infantry, volunteer; Roy, Lorenzo D., 11th Infantry, substitute.

Sands, Joseph, U. S. Navy, substitute; Sawyer, James A., unassigned, volunteer; Savage, Stephen D., 17th Infantry, drafted; Savage, Miner W., 12th Massachusetts; Scammon, George S., 11th Infantry, volunteer; Scates, Edgar, 20th Infantry, volunteer; Shaw, Resolvo, 20th Infantry, volunteer; Shepherd, Alfred, 21st Infantry, volunteer; Shepherd, Richard A., 19th Infantry, drafted; Sherburn, Jacob, 3rd Infantry, volunteer; Shorey, Chas. R., 20th Infantry, volunteer; Shorey, Chas. R., 3rd Infantry, volunteer; Sharp, Wm. J., 5th Battery; Simpson, Joseph D., 20th Infantry, volunteer; Small, Abner R., 3rd Infantry, volunteer; Smart, John M., 21st Infantry, volunteer; Smart, John M., Coast Guards, volunteer; Smiley, Albert R., 20th Infantry, volunteer; Smiley, Chas. N., 20th Infantry, volunteer; Smiley, Frank O., 3rd Infantry, volunteer; Smith, James P., 16th Infantry, volunteer; Smith, Lemuel H., 3rd Infantry, volunteer; Smith, Allen, V. S., volunteer; Soule, Martin B., 16th Infantry, volunteer; Soule, John W., 16th Massachusetts, volunteer; Soule, Josiah, 20th Infantry, volunteer; Soule, Daniel A., 20th Infantry, volunteer; Southard, Cyrus, 2nd Cavalry, volunteer; Spaulding, Nathan F., 15th Infantry, volunteer; Stevens, William A., 16th Infantry, volunteer; Stevens, Gilbert G., 26th Co. Infantry, unassigned; Stevens, Jason R., 7th Infantry, volunteer; Stevens, Wm. H., 20th Infantry, volunteer; Stevens, Edwin C., 16th Infantry, volunteer; Stuart, Chas. H., 31st Infantry, volunteer; Sturtevant, Reward A., 20th Infantry, volunteer.

Tallouse, John, 3rd Infantry, volunteer; Tallouse, Martin, 16th Infantry, volunteer; Thayer, Samuel J., 21st Infantry, volunteer; Thayer, Welcome, 3rd Infantry, volunteer; Thayer, Adin B., 16th Infantry, volunteer; Thing, Henry A., 3rd Infantry, volunteer; Thing, Chas. W., 1st Infantry, volunteer; Thing, Chas. W., 14th Infantry, volunteer; Thing, George S., 1st District of Columbia Cavalry and 1st Cavalry, volunteer; Thomas, John P. H., 2nd Cavalry, volunteer; Thomas, David S., 16th Infantry, volunteer; Thompson, James, 9th Infantry, volunteer; Thompson, Asa L., 4th Battery, volunteer; Thorn, James H., 1st District of Columbia Cavalry and 1st Cavalry, volunteer; Tilley, Geo. M., 31st Infantry, volunteer; Tozer, Henry M., 20th Infantry, volunteer; Tozier, Walter N., 30th Infantry, volunteer; Tozier, Albert F., 11th Infantry, volunteer; Tozier, Henry E., 8th Infantry, volunteer; Tracy, Geo. C., 5th Battery R. R.; Trask, Alexander, 21st Infantry, volunteer; Trask, Elbridge, Coast Guards, volunteer.

Vigue, Levi, 1st Cavalry, volunteer; Vigue, Levi, 31st Infantry, volunteer.

Ward, N. A., 17th Infantry, drafted; Watson, Andrew P., 21st Infantry, volunteer; Welch, Moses A., 31st Infantry, volunteer; Welch, James B., 1st District of Columbia Cavalry and 1st Cavalry, volunteer; Wells, Howard W., 16th Infantry, volunteer; West, Wallace W., 8th Infantry, volunteer; West, James O., 31st Infantry, volunteer; Wheeler, Geo. L., 3rd Infantry, volunteer; Wheeler, John N., 16th Infantry, volunteer; White, Henry, 1st Cavalry, volunteer; Williams, Andrew J., 14th Rhode Island Heavy Artillery, volunteer; Wilson, Geo. A. 21st Infantry, volunteer; Wilson, John B., 96th U. S. C. I., volunteer; Wingate, Henry, 14th Infantry, volunteer; Winslow, Hiram C., 21st Infantry, volunteer; Witham, Albert B., 4th Battery, volunteer; Woodbury, David, 3rd Uns. Co., R. R; Woodman, Alvin B., 3rd Infantry, volunteer; Woodman, Erastus W., 14th Infantry, United States Army, volunteer; Wyman, Wm. W., 3rd Infantry, volunteer; Wyman, Hiram, Coast Guards, volunteer; Wyman, Hiram R., 9th Infantry, volunteer; Wyman, Increase, 2nd Cavalry, volunteer; Wyman, W. W., 21st Infantry, volunteer; Wyman, Hiram, 21st Infantry, volunteer.

Young, Eugene H., 3rd Infantry, volunteer; Young, Roscoe G., 3rd Infantry, volunteer; Young, Eben W., 3rd Infantry, volunteer; Young, Laroy F., 30th Infantry, volunteer; Young, John M., 7th Infantry, volunteer.

Recapitulation.

Waterville furnished 525 soldiers during the Civil War, according to Adjutant-General's Report (page 24-1864-5) and yet the above list includes every name that can be found in town or State records, and numbers but 421.

The great discrepancy between these figures and the credits allowed this town by the Adjutant-General, occurs in several ways:

First: Many non-residents and foreigners were enlisted and credited on the town's quota whose enlistment papers would show some other residence, and would thus only count in the summary of town credits.

Second: A further discrepancy is caused by the commissioners of equalization refusing to credit the town; men originally placed to their credit, and in refusing to credit commissioned officers.

All calls for men by the President prior to July 2nd, 1862, were filled by voluntary enlistments, promiscuously; cities, towns and plantations not being called upon to furnish their proportional number of the State's allotment.

Men enlisting prior to July 2nd, 1862, were not credited upon the quota of any city or town in the State, but were simply placed upon the lists of names and classified to the cities and towns in which they resided.

Maine furnished more than her allotment of men under the President's calls in 1861 and had great difficulty in inducing the Government to accept two of her regiments of infantry and the 1st Maine Cavalry. Waterville furnished more than her share, but never received any credit for the excess.

Of the list furnished the commissioners of equalization by the municipal officers of Waterville, they allowed 171 three years men, 1 two years man, 50 one year men, 42 nine months men.

Making a total of 264 men subsequent to July 2, 1862, and allowed a credit for same of $19,883.33.

Third: The town secured an additional credit for each re-enlistment, while but one name appears for the two.

Fourth: The twenty-six "paper men" from Mr. ——— through J. P. Deering & Company, for which Joseph Percival,

1st selectman, paid $11,050, and ten "paper men" from Pike & Colby, for which Mr. Percival paid $4,250.

As this brings up the whole corruption of the "Paper credit" scandal, some explanation is necessary.

When the question of strengthening the armies of the Union was a simple one, of life or death with the Government, certain well known substitute brokers appeared in Augusta with lists of names which they claimed were those of men already in service not assigned to any quota.

These were offered to officers and agents of towns and municipalities of Maine who were looking for *men* to fill their quota and re-enforce our depleted Regiments. Where these substitute brokers obtained these lists of names;—by what villainous connivance and corruption the necessary authority was procured to enable the proper officers to certify officially to municipal officers on their quotas, hundreds of names of men who never existed,—without residence as required by law, without date of enlistment;—to certify even to two, ten or twenty recruits to a town without *any* names,—will never be known.

No one will ever know how much money the cities and towns of Maine were swindled out of by these ghouls of living and dead soldiers, because no one will ever know how many "paper men" were sold to them; but the commissioners, report "an aggregate of 1,380 after deducting the '251 list' said to have been *gratuitously distributed* by the Governor of Maine."

Mr. Pike, the member of Congress from the 5th District, speaking in the debate in the National House of Representatives in February, 1865, on this matter, said; "But worse than this:—credits have been given by these States when no men have *ever* been furnished, *anywhere, by anybody.*"

"Bold frauds!" "Paper men have been substituted for sailors, and up to this time 50% more sailors have been credited to the different states than there are in the Navy altogether."

Under date of Sept. 1st, 1864, Provost Marshal Gen. Frye, writes to Major Gardner, A. A. P. Marshal General at Augusta: "On examination of the records of the navy, I find only 158 men have been enlisted in the State of Maine during the Rebellion! I desire to call your attention to this fact;" and yet in December, same year, he approves and gives authenticity to the "251 list," *from one vessel,*—the Ohio.

In Provost Marshal General's criticism of our Commissioners' Report he writes: "It looks like sharp practice, to say the least of it, for the authorities in Maine to have sought and accepted paper credits and to have openly and voluntarily paid large sums of money to *scoundrels* for their part in preparing them."

This is one of the stereotyped excuses of the gang.

Speaking of the "251 list" of Mr. ————, the Committee say: "The men were not residents of Maine, or aliens enlisted here, and there was no law or general order by which they could be put to the credit of towns in Maine;" and again, "Perhaps it is fairly inferable from what we have of Mr. ————'s testimony, that he had some agency in procuring this 'Special Order.'

"It turned out that he had a very strong personal interest in procuring such, for he seems to have sold to Deering & Company, alone, 121 of these men (*names*) for $47,400; and if he sold the rest at the same rate, his gross sales must have amounted to more than $100,000." ("Paper Credits" by Hon. George F. Talbot and Gen. Selden Connor, Commissioners, under "Resolves of the Legislature" approved March 24, 1870.)

GOVERNMENT CALLS.

Under the President's call of April 15, 1861, for 75,000 militia for three months, the quota of Maine was 780; men furnished, 771.

Call of May 2, 1861, for 500,000 men, quota of Maine was 17,560; men furnished for three years, 18,104.

Call of July 2, 1862, for 300,000 men for three years, quota of Maine, 9,609; men furnished, 6,644.

Call of August 4, 1862, for 300,000 militia for nine months: Quota of Maine, 9,609; men furnished, 7,620.

Calls of October 17, 1863, (embracing men raised by draft of 1863) and February 1, 1864, for 500,000 for three years: Quota of Maine, 11,803; Men furnished, 11,958; paid commutation, 1,986; total, 13,944.

Call of March 14, 1864, for 200,000 men for three years; Quota of Maine, 4,721; men furnished, 7,042.

Call of July 18, 1864, for 500,000 men (reduced by excess of credits on previous calls) : Quota of Maine, 11,116; men furnished, 11,042; paid commutation, 11; total, 11,053.

Call of December 19, 1864, for 300,000 men: Quota of Maine, 8,389; men furnished, 6,936.

Under these eight calls there were furnished by the different states and territories more men than were ever put into the field by any nation in the history of the world, as will be seen by the following summary:

MEN FURNISHED DURING THE WAR.

(1)	Total number	2,778,304
	To army	2,672,341
	To navy	105,963
(2)	Estimated total number of re-enlistments	564,939
	In army	543,393
	In navy	21,546
(3)	Estimated total number of desertions	121,896
	From army	117,247
	From navy	4,649
(4)	Total number of deaths	364,116
	In army	359,528
	In navy	4,588
(5)	Estimated total number of individuals in service	2,213,365
	In army	2,128,948
	In navy	84,417
(6)	Estimated total number of survivors at termination of service (deserters excluded)	1,727,353
	In army	1,652,173
	In navy	75,180
	Estimated total number of survivors (deserters excluded) June 30, 1902	930,380
	Estimated average age of survivors at close of the war	28 years.

According to the mortality tables, 355,091 have died since 1890, and the average mortality will be about the same until the year 1925, although the percentage among the survivors rapidly increases.

In 1930 there will remain 37,033; in 1935 there will remain 6,296; in 1940 there will remain 340; in 1945 there will be no survivor of the War of the Rebellion.

TOTAL NUMBER OF MEN FURNISHED BY THE STATE OF MAINE DURING THE WAR.

In 1861.

15 Regiments Infantry, 1 Cavalry, 6 Batteries Mounted Artillery, 1 Company Sharpshooters, 3 Companies for Coast Fortifications, Recruits, etc..........	16,669

In 1862.

12 Regiments Infantry, 1 Regiment Heavy Artillery, Recruits, etc	15,690

In 1863.

2 Regiments Infantry, 2 Cavalry, 1 Battery of Artillery, Volunteers and Drafted men.................	10,223

In 1864-5.

2 Regiments Infantry, 30 Companies Unassigned Infantry, 6 Companies Sharpshooters, 3 Companies Coast Guards, Drafted men and Navy.........	30,363
	72,945

Maine sent this great army of her sons to the field, sealed with the traditions of their ancestors for courage and devotion; boys half of them, who passed straight from their mother's arms to the embrace of war.

There they left more than 7,000 of their number in known and unknown graves, among the hills and valleys of the South; buried where they fell; buried from the hospitals in camp and field or from the great hospitals of the cities, despite the devotion of heroic women; buried from the prison pens of the South, where they perished so miserably of exposure, starvation, delirium and despair; husbands, fathers, lovers, sons, comrades, friends; the patriotic, the brave, the true.

They are our uncalendared heroes. The language of their lives is written in the annals of our country. They helped with point of sword or bayonet to pen a chapter in American history that will be read while patriotism is honored or liberty cherished.

* * * * * * * * *

Lowell speaks of the heroes of the Civil War as marching
——"on a shining track
——heroes mustered in a gleaming row,
Beautiful evermore, and with the rays
Of morn on their white shields of expectation."

BOUNTIES.

The 1st Regiment of Infantry was enlisted for two years, though mustered into the United States service for three months only. The $22 bounty was paid to this organization. The 2nd Regiment of Infantry was enlisted and mustered into the United States service for two years, and received only the same State bounty as the 1st Regiment. Having originally some two hundred more men than the First, and recruits who enlisted when large bounties were paid, the aggregate amount of State bounty paid it, is much more than that to the First.

The 3rd, 4th, 5th, 6th, 7th, 8th, and 9th Regiments of Infantry were enlisted and mustered into the United States service for three years. They received the $22 State bounty at their muster into service. The re-enlisted men and some recruits of 1864 for those regiments received $300 State bounty. Recruits of 1862 and 1863 for those regiments received $55 State bounty.

The 10th Regiment was designed to be a re-organization of the 1st Regiment, which owed twenty-one months service to the government. The few men of the 1st Regiment who recognized their continuing liability to government under their enlistment, received no State bounty at the muster into United States service of this regiment; the remainder were paid the State bounty of $22. Fifty-five dollars State bounty was paid to recruits for three years service who were assigned to this regiment.

The 11th, 12th, 13th, 14th, and 15th Regiments of Infantry received no State bounty whatever. The amounts exhibited as paid to them were received by their recruits and re-enlisted men, in sums of from $55 to $300.

Th 16th, 17th, 18th, 19th and 20th Regiments of Infantry were paid a State bounty of $45. Recruits for these regiments were paid from $55 to $300 State bounty, except the 18th, which early ceased to exist as an infantry organization, and became the 1st Heavy Artillery, the recruits for which, as will be seen, were paid less than $100,000, mostly in $55 bounties.

The 21st, 22nd, 23rd, 24th, 25th, 26th, 27th and 28th Regiments of Infantry were enlisted and mustered into the United States service for nine months, and were paid no State bounty.

The 29th and 30th Regiments of Infantry received $100 State bounty.

The 31st and 32nd Regiments of Infantry were paid from $100 to $300 State bounty, their organization extending over the period during which these widely varying State bounties of from $100 to $300 were authorized. These regiments received but very few recruits. Two of the unassigned companies were incorporaed into the 31st Regiment.

The 1st Veteran Regiment of Infantry was composed largely of the recruits and re-enlisted men of the 5th, 6th and 7th Regiments of Infantry, who had received from $55 to $300 State bounty. Enlistments in this regiment proper were paid from $100 to $300 State bounty.

The 1st Regiment of Heavy Artillery is alluded to above.

The 1st Regiment of Cavalry was paid no State bounty at its muster into the United States service. The amount shown was paid its recruits and re-enlisted men in State bounties of from $55 to $300 each.

The 2nd Regiment of Cavalry was paid $100 State bounty, generally, though some few of the men received more. Its organization was commenced with a State bounty of $100, but before it was mustered into the United States service, $300 was authorized.

The 1st Regiment of D. C., or Baker's Cavalry, was being enlisted from the authorization of $55 bounties to those of $300, though most of the men were paid $100 State bounty.

The first six batteries of Mounted Artillery received no bounty from the State. Their recruits and re-enlisted men were paid from $55 to $300 State bounty.

The 7th Battery received from $100 to $300 State bounty.

Coast Guards and unassigned companies received from $100 to $300 State bounty. The most of these companies were assigned to regiments in the field.

Hancock's Corps received $100 State bounty.

1st Battalion Sharpshooters received from $100 to $300 State bounty.

Co. D, 2nd Regiment U. S. Sharpshooters, received $22 State bounty, and recruits and re-enlisted men from $55 to $300 each. United States' organizations, and those of other states, received from $55 to $300 State bounty.

The State paid for actual naval enlistments made subsequent to February 2, 1864, of our own citizens duly credited to localities in this State, bounties of $100, $200 and $300, for one, two, or three years' service, except as stipulated in order of November, 1864, confirmed by subsequent statute, that not exceeding $100 should be paid for any period of enlistment not less than one year, if place of recruit's credit had filled all calls without him. This order also applied to enlistments for land service in Maine organizations, as also for those of the government and other states.

All these State bounty payments were made only for new bona fide enlistments, when the enlistment contract, and descriptive and muster-in-rolls were duly filed in the adjutant general's office, and when entering organizations other than those of Maine volunteers, in addition to the foregoing papers, the place of credit in this State was duly certified by the proper officer having official knowledge of the enlistment and credit.

Citizens of this State enlisted in the navy to the credit of localities herein, subsequent to February 2, 1864, though credited only by the "commission," were paid State bounty under the statute if, in addition to the receipts in duplicate invariably required, the enlistment and other papers above specified were filed in the adjutant general's office. It will be observed that a smaller amount of State bounty was paid the original members of the entire first ten regiments of infantry and company of sharpshooters, the most of whom were mustered into United States service for three years, than was received by a single regiment

of infantry two years later for a like enlistment, but a shorter
period of service as eventually proved. The original members
of thirteen regiments of infantry, one regiment of cavalry, and
six batteries of mounted artillery, were paid no State bounty.
The original members of five regiments of infantry received $45
each. The entire State bounties paid the original members of
twenty-eight of our infantry regiments, from the 1st to the 28th
inclusive, the 1st Cavalry, and first six batteries of Mounted
Artillery, amounted to only about $400,000. All of the re-enlisted men of those organizations (some 4,000 in number received
$300 each, State bounty, and some of them a large local bounty
in addition thereto, although the same was prohibited by the
statute. Many members of the eight regiments for nine months'
service are found among the recruits of old regiments in 1864,
and received liberal State and local bounties. The same is found
to be the case with members of the two "two years" regiments,
and a large number of those of other regiments of 1861 and 1862,
who were discharged for disability, and upon their recovery
enlisted into our old and new organizations and were paid liberal
bounties.

THE PERIOD OF THE WAR.

It is not generally known that the War of the Rebellion did not
begin or close at the same time in all the states. The dates of
the commencement and the termination of that war indicated in
the opinion of the supreme court of the United States in the case
of "The Protector" which is reported in 12 Wallace, 700,
and is in substance, that the proclamation of the intended blockade by the President may be assumed as marking the first of
these dates, and the proclamation that the war had closed, as
marking the second.

There were two proclamations of intended blockade; the first
of the 19th of April, 1861, embracing the states South Carolina,
Georgia, Alabama, Florida, Mississippi, Louisiana, and Texas;—
the second of the 27th of April, 1861, embracing the states of
Virginia and North Carolina;—and there were two proclamations declaring that the war had closed;—one issued on the 2nd
of April, 1866, embracing the states of Virginia, North Caro-

lina, South Carolina, Georgia, Florida, Mississippi, Tennessee, Alabama, Louisiana, and Arkansas, and the other issued on the 20th of August, 1866, embracing the state of Texas.

In the absence of more certain criteria, of equally general application we must take the dates of these proclamations as determining the commencement and the close of the war in the states mentioned in them.

WATERVILLE SOLDIERS' MONUMENT ASSOCIATION.

Many of our citizens still living will recall the terrible days of the war; when battle was on and victory hung in the balance; when care for the sick and wounded, and honoring the dead, was the duty and desire of all the living,—that even then a few of our patriotic citizens inaugurated a plan to raise funds for the erection of a suitable monument to perpetuate the memory of our dead soldiers.

The inception and successful prosecution of this plan is due to the patriotism and untiring energy of Mr. G. A. Phillips, as to him more than any man living here to-day or who has ever lived here is due the present prosperity of Waterville.

The following facts, copied from the records of the Waterville Monument Association, will interest our older citizens, and should interest the younger.

"On the evening of the 14th of March, 1864, a concert was given in this village, the proceeds of which, by previous announcement, were to be donated in aid of erecting a suitable monument to the memory of our soldiers who had fallen in defence of the Union, or who should thereafter lose their lives in the same patriotic service.

The names of these performers, which all will agree should appear upon the first page of this record, were: Mrs. J. E. Dow, Miss A. M. Bates, Miss C. M. Barney, Miss L. S. Carroll, Miss E. Piper, Miss H. C. Marston, Miss S. E. Ransted, Mr. Wm. A. Caffrey, Mr. S. C. Marston, Mr. J. R. Pitman, Mr. G. A. Phillips.

During the intermission, a proposition to form a permanent organization for the more speedy and certain accomplishment of the work was introduced; and after some explanations and discussion, a committee was chosen to prepare a plan of organization, to be submitted at a future meeting, with a list of officers, etc. The following gentlemen were put upon this committee:

J. Nye, J. B. Foster, G. A. Phillips, E. G. Meader, and C. M. Morse.

A second concert in aid of this object was given by the same individuals on the evening of the 23rd of the same month, at which time the committee named above reported a constitution, which was unanimously adopted. The following list of candidates was also presented, and after the adoption of the constitution, they were chosen to the several offices for which they were severally designated.

G. A. Phillips, president; Wm. A. Caffrey, vice-president; Daniel R. Wing, secretary; Geo. L. Robinson, treasurer; Jones R. Elden, E. G. Meader, C. M. Morse, trustees.

Article 2 of the constitution reads as follows: "The object of this association shall be to procure the erection, at such time and in such place within the town as shall hereafter be designated, of a suitable monument in honor of those of our fellow-citizens, residents of Waterville, who shall have died in the military or naval service of the United States during the present war."

Appended to the constitution are the names of ninety-two persons.

A second benefit concert was given in 1865 and efforts were made to secure a contribution of one dollar from each citizen for the association.

* * * * * * * * *

Here occurs a hiatus of nearly ten years, or from November 29, 1865, to June 14, 1875, during which there is no record of any kind, nor any explanation of the interregnum.

There were doubtless good reasons, and the first that suggests itself is the effervescence of zeal, as this has occurred in the history of many commemorative monuments; but the *purpose* was fixed in the minds of good men and the funds drawing interest.

* * * * * * * * *

In 1875 the fund with accumulated interest amounted to $1,000, this with the $1,000 voted by the town made $2,000 available for the purpose of the association. The meeting of the association at which such report was made was *the last meeting*

BREVET BRIG. GEN. FRANCIS E. HEATH.

held in the old town hall before it was remodeled. This fact Secretary Daniel R. Wing thought was worthy of permanent record. The committee to submit plans and estimates for a monument was as follows: Col. F. E. Heath, Dr. Atwood Crosby, Edwin Noyes, Reuben Foster, J. H. Plaisted.

This committee recommended the purchase of Milmore's "Citizen Soldier" in bronze, the price to be $2,000. This recommendation was accepted and a committee consisting of the officers of the association, Edwin Noyes, Col. I. S. Bangs and J. H. Plaisted, was appointed to procure a suitable monument upon which to place the statue.

The committee to locate the monument consisted of Nathaniel Meader, E. R. Emerson, Miss Florence Plaisted, Miss Roxana Hanscom, Dr. Crosby and Mrs. Crosby, C. G. Carleton, M. C. Foster, C. K. Mathews, C. R. McFadden, F. P. Haviland, P. S. Heald, Reuben Foster, W. B. Arnold, Prof. E. W. Hall, Prof. M. Lyford, A. A. Plaisted and Mrs. Plaisted, Dr. N. R. Boutelle and Mrs. Boutelle, E. B. Cummings, E. F. Webb and the officers of the association.

The following inscriptions were accepted. On the Elm street front, "To the memory of the Soldiers and Sailors of Waterville who gave their lives for the preservation of the Republic 1861-1865." On the opposite front, "Erected by the citizens of Waterville."

In order to raise the balance of the money needed for the monument the ladies of the committee decided to have an entertainment on two evenings, the 16th and 17th of May, 1876, the first evening to consist of an antiquarian supper and concert; the second of music, tableaux, free lunch, presentation of flag to G. A. R. Post, by the ladies, etc. And this was ratified by the association.

The entertainments were a grand success, in every way, and will be long remembered with pleasure by those present. A full account will be found in the Mail of May 19, 1876. Three hundred and fifty dollars were added to the funds of the association.

The Waterville Soldiers' Monument was dedicated with appropriate ceremonies on Memorial day, Tuesday, May 30, 1876. Col. F. E. Heath acted as marshal; the Waterville brass band furnished the music; the members of W. S. Heath Post, G. A. R., joined in the procession, with Waterville 3 Engine Company, Ticonic 1, Appleton Hook and Ladder Company and the Colby Rifles did escort duty. These formed in procession on the Common, and with the officers of the association in carriages and citizens following, marched through the streets to Monument Park, where prayer was offered by Rev. C. D. Crane; a financial statement and the Roll of Honor were read by Mr. G. A. Phillips, the president; the monument was unveiled; an oration delivered by Mr. L. Stevens, Esq., of Portland; a poem read by A. L. Hinds, Esq., of Benton, and a hymn sung by a select choir.

The Roll of Honor, deposited beneath the monument, with a list of the officers, etc., is as follows:

Benjamin C. Allen, William H. Aderton, Charles R. Atwood, David Bates, Charles Bowen, William H. Bowen, Elijah Ballantyne, George W. Bowman, Jr., Joseph Oren Brackett, Bennett Bickford, George A. E. Blake, William Barrett, Hiram Cochran, Alonzo Copp, William Chapman, Isaac W. Clark, Charles Clark, Lorenzo D. Clark, Albert Corson, William H. DeWolfe, Octavius A. Davis, Hadley P. Dyer, Stephen Ellis, Dighton Ellis, Pawlette Euarde, Charles A. Farrington, Hiram Fish, Thomas A. Gibbs, David B. Gibbs, George C. Getchell, Edward B. Herbert, William S. Heath, William H. Ham, Algernon P. Herrick, Albro Hubbard, Joseph Jerow, John O. James, Moses King, Charles F. Lyford, William H. Marston, Alvin Messer, John N. Messer, Orren Messer, Lewis Murray, Joseph M. Penney, William W. Penney, Pelatiah Penney, Ira D. Penney, Richard Perley, William H. Phelps, James B. Pullen, Henry Pooler, Edwin Plummer, Edward E. Prescott, Albert Quimby, James F. Ricker, Peter Roderick, Miner W. Savage, Joseph D. Simpson, Richard A. Shepherd, W. A. Stevens, Edwin C. Stevens, Gilbert G. Stevens, Jason R. Stevens, Adin B. Thayer, George Tilley, Martin Tallow, Henry E. Tozier, Wallace W. West, James O. West, Erastus D. Woodman, George L. Wheeler, John M. Wheeler, Henry White, William W. Wyman, Eben W. Young, Roscoe G. Young. (The name of Wm. H. Bacon should have been added to this list as he died here in 1862). (I. S. B.)

The financial statement submitted by President Phillips read as follows: "We have received from all sources, since our association was organized, $2,772.84; we have expended for filling and grading, $76.90; for plans for pedestal, $25.00; for freight on statue, $16.18; for pedestal, including foundation, $982.75; for bronze statue, $1,600.00; total expenditure, $2,700.83; balance in treasury, $72.01.

DANIEL R. WING, *Secretary*.

The number of persons who were members of the Monument Association was 239.

W. S. HEATH POST NO. 14, DEPARTMENT OF MAINE, G. A. R.

The Grand Army of the Republic was founded by Dr. B. F. Stevenson of Springfield, Ill., in 1866.

Dr. Stevenson devoted the best years of his life to his grand idea of a brotherhood of old soldiers, to perpetuate the memories of the camp, the march and the battlefield, and to perpetuate the memory and history of the dead. Could he have lived to see the day, what a tribute to his prophetic vision, what a reward for his labor, would have been the increasing numbers of his comrades till they reached the high water mark of 400,000 in 1888 to 1892; these recruited from the men who served as citizen soldiers and as soldier citizens with equal credit in war and peace!

The Grand Army of the Republic symbolizes fraternity, charity and loyalty. It stands for American manhood. It epitomizes the heroism of a Nation. It is the trustee of patriotism.

Memorial Day is their creation and they who love liberty must succeed them in their annual pilgrimage to the shrines of their dead when their last member shall have passed beyond our feeble following.

W. S. Heath Post, No. 14, Department of Maine, G. A. R., was organized in 1874 and chartered December 29th of the same year, under the administration of Department Commander General Seldon Connor, with the following charter members: * Atwood Crosby, * F. E. Heath, I. S. Bangs, * J. H. Plaisted, O. F. Mayo, * Levi A. Dow, A. P. Webb, * Addison Dolly, * Sidney Keith, Redford M. Estes, Alpheus S. Webber, John U. Hubbard, George W. Hubbard, Henry J. Goulding, George W. Goulding, E. P. Buck, W. H. Emery, W. H. Russell, R. T. Beazley, * G. A. Osborne, James W. King, * Moses J. Kelley, * Charles W. Lowe, E. N. Small, G. T. Stevens, A. M. Sawtelle.

The Post was named by these veterans after Lieutenant Colonel W. S. Heath of the 5th Maine Infantry, who was killed at the battle of Gaines Mill.

Its first commander was General * Francis E. Heath, and he was succeeded by General I. S. Bangs, Dr. * Atwood Crosby, G. H. Mathews, Captain * Charles Bridges, A. O. Libby, * J. G. Stover, Dr. D. P. Stowell, N. S. Emery, George W. Reynolds, S. S. Vose, George A. Wilson, P. S. Heald, J. L. Merrick, F. D. Lunt, E. Gilpatrick, A. E. Ellis, Captain J. P. Garland, J. H. Coombs, O. P. Richardson, Captain Silas Adams, H. C. Proctor, and J. R. Pollard.

The Post has on its roll of membership 195 names.

Death, emigration, and other causes have reduced its membership to fifty-seven, but it is still one of the vigorous, active Posts of the order, and is doing a noble charitable work, looking with great fidelity after the necessities of sick and disabled comrades, their widows and orphans, whether members of their organization or not.

If it performed no other duty, it would commend itself to the charitable and humane, but in a higher sphere of influence, it is an organized exemplar of loyalty, by the service of its members to the land they helped to save, and a *lesson* in loyalty to the generation that are to follow them.

January 30, 1891, Hon. Nahaniel Meader, then Mayor of the city of Waterville, presented to the Post a very beautiful record book, especially designed for recording the name and military history of its members.

It has taken the writer and Comrade A. O. Libbey of the committee, five or six years to secure the names and record of 105 of these members from Waterville and Winslow, verify them, have them re-written and engrossed in the great book.

The labors of the committee are finished, and the record—the lasting memorial to her patriotic sons, is to be presented to the city of Waterville as soon as a depository is provided for its safe keeping.

The Post has had leading place and influence in all observances of a patriotic character, has made its campfires schools of

---
* Deceased

patriotism, has furnished to the Department of Maine, Commander Gen. I. S. Bangs and Commander James L. Merrick. It has pleasant headquarters in Masonic block which are always open. The Woman's Relief Corps has added greatly to the comfort and efficiency of the Post.

Since its organization, the Post has paid its annual tribute of respect to the memory of dead comrades whose graves are within its jurisdiction in Waterville and Winslow.

The number of these is so rapidly augmenting, that they already number nearly three times the Post membership, and will increase until all have joined the ranks of the great army of the dead, to take up their march under the loving eye and guiding hand, to which we confidently commit them.

THE REVOLUTIONARY WAR.

The Revolutionary War commenced with the battle of Lexington, April 19, 1775. Provisional articles of peace were signed, November 30, 1782, and proclamation of cessation of hostilities ordered by the Continental Congress, April 11, 1783. Definite treaty of peace was concluded, September 3, 1783, ratified by the Continental Congress and proclaimed, January 14, 1784.

From a report of the Secretary of War to the House of Representatives, dated May 10, 1790, and published in American State Papers, Military Affairs, Volume I, pages 14 to 19, it appears that the number of troops and militia furnished from time to time by the several states during the Revolutionary War was 395,330. It is impossible to ascertain whether the figures, which are given in the report for each year of the war, and which aggregate 395,330 for the whole period of the war, represent only the number of new enlistments each year, or whether they include not only men who enlisted during each year but also those who were in the service at some time during that year but who enlisted during a prior year. In other words, it cannot be determined positively whether the figures for each year merely represent *additions* to the force during that year, or whether they represent these additions together with the force *remaining in service from a prior year.* It is certain that, in either case, they do not represent the total number of individuals in service in any year, or the total number of individuals added to the force in any year, because there must have been many duplications caused by counting the same man over again for each successive enlistment. It is well known that a very large proportion of the men who served in the American army during the Revolutionary War rendered two, three or more terms, or "tours" of service. This was notably the case in militia organizations in which men frequently served tours of a few days each at comparatively short intervals.

The writer feels it unnecessary to apologize for the meager incidents that serve to connect this generation with events of a century and more ago.

The time for detail was passed when the old Revolutionary soldiers passed away and their families were separated.

Their military history was carefully preserved by the Commonwealth of Massachusetts, and if identity could be established, a biographical sketch might be written that would confer credit upon the soldier and his biographer.

The writer presents the most and the best sketch of these old worthies possible who went from Waterville (then Winslow) or came here after the war and found a home and a final resting place here or in the immediate vicinity.

RECORDS OF SERVICE IN THE REVOLUTION.

Captain Dean Bangs, grandfather of Isaac Sparrow Bangs, was born May 31, 1756, in Harwich (now Brewster), Cape Cod, Mass. He married April 21, 1780, Eunice Sparrow, daughter of Isaac, son of Jonathan, son of Jonathan, son of Jonathan, who married Hannah, daughter of Gov. Thomas Prence and Patience, daughter of Elder Brewster.

He "followed the sea" as boy and man for forty years; became mate and master in the East India trade, was a privateer in the first year of the War of the Revolution, and then enlisted in Abijah Bangs' company, Colonel Dike's regiment in 1776 and served two years.

In 1802 he came to Sidney and bought a large tract of land on the Kennebec river and there lived and reared a large family. Waterville was his mercantile home and here he raised a company of artillery during the War of 1812 for Major Joseph Chandler's Battalion of Artillery, and marched to Augusta with the other companies of the Waterville contingent. He died, December 6, 1845, and was buried in a private cemetery on his own farm in a beautiful spot overlooking the Kennebec river, where lie several of his family, including his wife and one son.

The cemetery is enclosed by a permanent granite and iron fence, and in this enclosure near Captain Bangs' grave is a cenotaph in memory of his father, whose military record is inscribed as follows:

To the memory of
ELKANAH BANGS,
(father of Dean Bangs),

who was in the privateer service of the Revolution; was taken prisoner with three of his neighbors, and died on board the Jersey prison ship at Wallabout Bay, New York, in July, 1777, aged 44 years; this

CENOTAPH

is respectfully dedicated by his great-grandson, Isaac Sparrow, son of Isaac Sparrow, son of Dean Bangs, who settled upon this farm in the year 1802.

Thomas Bates: Corporal, Capt. John Gibb's Co., Col. Ebenezer Sprout's Regt.; service from December 8 to December 10, 1776, two days, marched to Falmouth on an alarm at Elizabeth Islands: Roll dated at Wareham:

Also, Private Capt. Samuel Brigg's Co., Col. Theophilis Cotton's Regt., General Palmer's Brigade; service 32 days on a secret expedition to Tiverton, R. I., September 29, 1777. (Do. Vol. I, page 803.)

Also, Capt. Gibb's Co. (4th Plymouth), Col. Sprout's Regt., service from September 6 to September 10, 1778, 5 days, marched to Dartmouth on an alarm:

Also, pay roll for five days' service from September 13, 1778, marched to Falmouth on an alarm:

Also, Capt. Gibb's (4th Plymouth) Co., Lt.-Col. White's Regt.

Thomas Bates: Enlisted July 31, 1780, discharged August 9, 1780, service nine days at Rhode Island: Roll sworn to at Wareham. (Ibid. Vol. I, page 804).

Thomas Bates: Sergeant, Capt. Joseph Parker's Co., Col. Ebenezer Sprout's Regiment: Muster roll dated February 13, 1778: Enlisted January 9, 1778, enlisted for three months from January 1, 1778; stationed at Rhode Island.

Also, Capt. John Gibb's Co., Col. John Jacobs' Regiment: Enlisted July 23, 1780, discharged October 27, 1780; service three months, six days on an alarm at Rhode Island: Enlistment three months; company raised to reinforce Continental Army: Roll dated Wareham. (Ibid. Vol. I, page 804.)

Was a pensioner and lived in Waterville in 1840. Date of death, and burial place unknown.

John Cole: Appears with rank of *Private* (on Continental Army pay accounts, Captain Redding's company, 5th) in Col. Bradford's regiment for service from March 8, 1777, to December 31, 1779. Residence, Winslow, Me. Vol. :14 :2 :74.

He appears with rank of *Private* on Continental Army pay accounts of Capt. Haskell's company, Col. Bradford's regiment, for service from January 1, 1780, to March 8, 1780. Residence, Winslow. Vol. :14 :1 :35.

He appears in Capt. John Samont's company, Colonel Gamaliel Bradford's (15th) regiment Massachusetts line from Winslow. Was pensioned in 1818. He moved to Albion about 1814 and died there January 11, 1824. His age unknown, but probably less than seventy years. His widow, Polly Cole, on papers signed by her July 7, 1835, alleges her age then as seventy-one.

John Cool: Appears with rank of *Private* on Continental Army pay accounts of Capt. Sewell's company, Colonel Sprout's regiment for service from March 12, 1777, to December 31, 1779. Residence, Winslow, also given in Capt. Josiah Jenkins company, Col. Brewer's regiment, dated, Camp near Valley Forge, January 23, 1778. Vol. :12 :2 :79 :10 :319.

Was discharged at Fishkill, N. Y., March 12th, 1780, having served full three years; his term of enlistment. He alleged on a paper dated May 26, 1835, that he was then seventy-eight years old and had lived in Waterville (Winslow) seventy years. He lived on Cool street, which after his death was named for him. He died October 5, 1845, aged eighty-nine years, six months, and was buried in the old cemetery and afterwards removed to Pine Grove cemetery.

Levi Crowell: Born, reared and enlisted on Cape Cod. After the war drifted "down east" to Winslow (that part in which is now Oakland) with Elisha and Solomon Hallett. Date of death unknown. Buried in old cemetery, Oakland.

Manoah Crowell: Was pensioned in 1834 for service in the Massachusetts militia, but his name is not to be found in Massachusetts records. He was said to be seventy-one years old in 1835, but is put down at seventy-eight in 1840, when he was living in Waterville (now Oakland) and drawing his pension there.

The date of his death is unknown, but he was a soldier in the War of 1812.

John Davis: Appears with rank of *private* on muster roll of Capt. Jeremiah Hill's company, Col. Scammon's regiment, dated August 1, 1775. Enlisted May 5, 1775. Time of service, twelve weeks, four days. Residence, Biddeford. Eight month's service. Vol. 15, p. 28.

He appears with rank of *drummer* on company return of Capt. Hill's company, Col. Scammon's regiment (30th), dated September 27, 1775. Enlisted May 5, 1775. Residence, Biddeford. Coat Rolls. Eight months' service. Vol. 56, p. 199.

He appears among signatures to an order for bounty coat or its equivalent in money, due for the eight months' service in Capt. Jeremiah Hill's company, Col. James Scammon's regiment, dated October 6, 1775. Coat Rolls. Vol. 57, File 21.

He appears with rank of *drummer* on muster roll of Capt. Jeremiah Hill's company, Col. Edmund Phinney's regiment, dated in garrison, Fort George, December 8, 1776. Enlisted January 1, 1776. Re-enlisted November 14, 1776. Vol. 46, p. 3.

During the winter months of 1776 he enlisted for the war and served as drummer and drum-major in Col. Joseph

Vose's (First) Regiment, Massachusetts Line, and was discharged in June, 1783. He was five feet, six inches high, light complexion, light hair. He claimed to have been in the Battle of Monmouth and at the surrender of Burgoyne, and to have marched to Yorktown and been present at the surrender of Cornwallis. He was at one time reported as a deserter, but the charge was cancelled and this record removed.

He came to New Sharon in 1794 and to Waterville about 1830. He had nine children, but never owned any property in New Sharon or Waterville. He was probably a skilled mechanic.

Mr. Davis was born in Simbross, Cork county, Ireland, about 1754. The date of his death and place of burial are unknown, but he was living here in 1835, and at his great age would hardly return to New Sharon. He died before 1840, if he died here, as, although he was a pensioner, he was not on the list of fifteen living here and in Winslow in 1840.

Oliver Dow, and his cousin Amos, enlisted in Captain Watts' company in Salem, N. H., in 1756. Oliver continued in same company in Colonel N. Meserve's regiment; fought at Crown Point, Ticonderoga, and in other campaigns.

In 1777 he was in Captain Joseph Bailey's company, Moses Kelly's regiment, General Whipple's brigade.

In 1781 he served in Captain Nathaniel Head's company of Lieut.-Col. David Reynolds' regiment of New Hampshire troops.

He was a lieutenant as early as 1776, as appears from military archives, his name appearing with other Hopkinton men.

Oliver Dow was born in Salem, N. H., in 1736; moved to Hopkinton in 1773, back to Salem about 1790, and lived there 'till 1820, when he moved to Waterville with his son Levi, died here December 18, 1824, and was buried in Monument Park.

He was grandfather of Charles Dow who lived and died here, and great- grandfather of Levi A. Dow, late of Co. B, 21st Maine Infantry Volunteers.

He was a great-grandfather of Hon. Richard S. Dow, counsellor-at-law, State street, Boston, Mass., to whom the writer is indebted for this biographical sketch.

Sampson Freeman: Appears in a return of men enlisted into the Continental Army from 1st Essex county regiment. Residence, Salem. Term, three years. Joined Capt. Fairfield's company, Col. Wigglesworth's regiment. Vol. 41, p. 44.

Appears with rank of *private* on muster roll of Capt. Joseph McNall's company, Col. Edward Wigglesworth's regiment. Dated Camp at Valley Forge, June 2, 1778. Term three years. Vol. 61, p. 24.

Appears with rank of *private* on muster and pay roll of Capt. Peter Page's company, Col. Wigglesworth's regiment, for March and April, 1779, dated at Providence, May 5, 1779. Enlisted February 1, 1777, three years. Transferred to Capt. John K. Smith's company, Col. Smith's regiment. Vol. 22, p. 98.

Appears with rank of *private* on Continental Army pay accounts of Capt. John K. Smith's company, Col. Smith's regiment, for service from February 1, 1777, to February 5, 1780. Residence, Salem. Continental Army books.

Sampson Freeman was a free man of color who came to Waterville from Peru, Me., in 1835, and after a brief acquaintance married Venus, the widow of Prince Henry, who lived on the second rangeway and owned a small farm. Venus was brought up in the family of Judge Redington of Vassalboro. Her husband must have died before 1825, as she was a widow in 1826, and lived on the farm she inherited from him and which is now a part of the farm of J. C. Blaisdell on the 2nd rangeway. Freeman lived with "Aunt Venus" six years, when she died and was buried in Monument Park. He died in 1843 and was buried near her.

Enoch Fuller, Revolutionary soldier, died in Winslow, January 29, 1842, aged eighty-seven, and was buried in the "Old Fort" Cemetery.

Seth Getchell: Grandfather of Miss Julia Stackpole, enlisted from Berwick, Maine, where he was born in 1753. He married Sarah Grant, by whom he had nine children, all of whom are dead.

He came here soon after the close of the Revolutionary War, owned a small farm about two and a half miles west of Waterville village, and worked in a grist mill, which might have been near the dam of the Union Gas & Electric Co., on the Messalonskee or farther up that stream at the Rice bridge. In 1840 he lived with Susan Stackpole.

He died in Pittsfield, Maine, in July, 1845, aged ninety-one years, eight months. His wife survived him, but died in February of the following year, and the remains of both were brought here and buried in Pine Grove Cemetery.

Nathaniel Gilman: Has record of service but no way to identify him positively, as there are many of the same name. He lived here and died here before 1840, as his widow, Sarah Gilman, was a pensioner here at that date. The date of his birth, death or place of enlistment are in doubt, but he was buried in the family vault in the old cemetery, and when it was made into a park (Monument) the vault was demolished and all the bodies removed to Pine Grove Cemetery.

Elisha Hallett: Private, Capt. Elisha Nye's company. Enlisted February 14, 1776; service to November 21, 1776, nine months, six days. Company stationed at Elizabeth Islands for defense of sea coast, *also,* Capt. Elisha Hedge's company, Col. Freeman's regiment. Enlisted September 3, 1779. Discharged September 18, 1779; service five days. Company detached for military service at Falmouth on an alarm. Massachusetts Soldiers and Sailors in Revolution, Vol. VII, p. 122.

Received a pension; lived in Waterville, in 1840, at the age of eighty-two years, with Jonathan Hallet. Date of death unknown; buried in old cemetery in Oakland.

Solomon Hallett: Private, Capt. Joshua Gray's company.* Enlisted November 1, 1775, discharged December 31, 1775, service two months, five days in defense of sea coast. Roll dated Barnstable.

* Capt. Joshua Gray of Yarmouth; captain of a company of minute-men, engaged July 1, 1775, discharged December 31, 1775.

Private, Capt. Ebenezer Baker's company, Col. Freeman's regiment. Marched, October 4, 1777, service eighteen days. Company marched to Tiverton, R. I., on a secret expedition.

Private, Capt. Micah Hamlen's company, Col. Jonathan Reed's (1st) regiment of Guards. Marched, April 2, 1778. Service to July 6, 1778, three months, four days, at Cambridge, including four days (eighty miles) travel home. Enlistment three months from April 2, 1778.

Private, Capt. Elisha Hedge's company,* Col. Freeman's regiment. Marched September 3, 1779. Discharged September 18, 1779. Service fifteen days. Company detached from militia for service at Falmouth on an alarm.

* Capt. Elisha Hedge, Yarmouth, Capt. 2nd (1st Yarmouth) company, 1st Barnstable County Regiment of Massachusetts Militia.

Solomon Hallett was living in Waterville (now Oakland) in 1840, at the age of eighty-six, and was a pensioner. He died soon after this date and was buried in the old cemetery at West Waterville (now Oakland).

Timothy Littlefield: Enlisted from Wells, Maine, September 4, 1775, in Capt. Noah Moulton Littlefield's company, and served three months and fifteen days at Wells and Arundell, guarding sea coast.

Also: In Capt. James Littlefield's company, Col. Stover's regiment from August 14, 1777, to November 14, 1777, four months and three days, including 300 miles travel home from Coeman's (Queman's (?) Heights with Northern Army.

Also: Served to reinforce the Continental Army from August 2, 1780, to December 26, 1780, five months and nine days, including fifteen days' travel home.

Descriptive list, 6' 1" high, light complexion, age twenty-one years.

Was a pensioner and lived here in 1840. Date of death and place of interment unknown.

Salathiel Penny: Appears with rank of *private* on muster roll of Capt. Samuel Sayer's company, Col. James Scammon's regiment, dated August 1, 1775. Time of service three months, four days. Enlisted May 3, 1775. Residence, Wells, eight months' service. Vol. 16, p. 27.

Appears with rank of *private* on company return of Capt. Samuel Sayer's company, Col. James Scammon's regiment, October, 1775. Enlisted May 3, 1775. Residence, Wells, Me. Coat Rolls, eight months' service. Vol. 56, p. 205.

Appears among signatures to an order for bounty coat or its equivalent in money due for the eight months' service in 1775, in Capt. Samuel Sayer's company, Col. James Scammon's (30th) regiment, dated Cambridge, October 27, 1775. Coat Rolls, Vol. 57, File 21.

Appears with rank of *private* on muster roll of Capt. Silas Wild's company, Col. Edmund Phinney's regiment, dated in Garrison at Fort George, December, 1776. Enlisted January 10, 1776. Time of service, ten months, four days. Reported sick in barracks. Re-engaged. November 14, 1776, under Col. Brewer. Vol. 46, p. 6.

Salathiel Penny: Appears with rank of private on muster and pay roll of Capt. Daniel Merrill's company, Col. Samuel Brewer's regiment. Marched to Bennington. Enlisted January 1, 1777. Was present at the surrender of Burgoyne. Discharged March 17, 1777. Residence, Wells. Vol. 21, p. 100.

Was born in Wells, Maine, in 1756. First wife unknown; second wife was Margaret C. Grant of Berwick.

Mr. Penney settled upon and cleared the farm where he lived and died, and which is now owned by Mrs. Moses Penney.

By his first wife he had two daughters and one son. Peletiah, father of William G. Penney, father of our "Penney Boys," Ira, Peletiah, Charles, William and Fred and one daughter, Harriet, who married Nelson McCrillis.

Salathiel Penney died September 22, 1847, aged ninety-one years, and was buried in Monument Park. About 1875 his remains were removed to Pine Grove Cemetery.

John Pullen: Was born at Attleboro, Mass., May 7, 1763. He was the youngest of the nine children of James Pullen and Lydia Woodcock, his wife, who had been married at Attleboro, February 26, 1742. Lydia Woodcock was the daughter of Jonathan Woodcock, who is said to have been a very brave man and of much influence in the colony at that time.

John's grandfather and the father of James was Nicholas Pullen. He is the earliest ancestor that the family have thus far been able to find, and nothing is known of him except the fact of his marriage at Rehoboth, Mass., on January 19, 1709, to Mary Tucker.

John Pullen was a Revolutionary soldier, his name appearing in a descriptive list of men raised to reinforce the Continental army for the term of six months agreeably to a resolve of June 5, 1780. He is there described as seventeen years of age, five feet, four inches in height and of dark complexion. His residence is given as Attleboro. He arrived at Springfield, July 9, 1780, and with the 11th Division, to which this re-enforcement was assigned, marched to camp, July 11, 1780, under command of Ensign Barrows. (Mass. Muster and Pay Rolls. Vol. 35, page 192.)

The name of John Pullen of Attleboro also appears in a return dated Camp Totoway, October 25, 1780, containing a list of men raised for six months' service and returned by Brig.-Gen. Patterson as having passed muster. (Mass. Muster and Pay Rolls, Vol. 25, page 241.)

He was in the Continental army from July 6, 1780 to January 8, 1781, having seen six months' and two days' service.

John Pullen was married at Winthrop, Me., June 23, 1785, to Amy Bishop, daughter and youngest child of Squire Bishop and Patience Titus. Eight children were born of this union, one of whom, Sarah Boardman, married John Caffrey, who was the grandfather of Mrs. L. D. Carver of Augusta.

John Pullen died March 29, 1810, at the age of forty-seven, at Waterville, Me., and was buried in the old cemetery on Elm street, now Monument Park.

His widow, Amy Bishop Pullen, resided for a number of years in Waterville with her daughter, Mrs. Sarah Boardman Caffrey, and was living as late as the year 1836, when she made application for State bounty, as appears by the records in the land office of Maine.

Asa Redington: Was born in the town of Boxford, Essex Co., Mass., December 22, 1761. Son of Abraham and Sarah (Kimball) Redington. In June, 1778 he enlisted in Wilton, N. H., in Col. Peabody's regiment, and joined the forces of Gen. Sullivan at Providence, R. I., where the troops were quartered in Brown College.

In December he was discharged and returned to Wilton, N. H. In June, 1779, re-enlisted in the "Continental Establishment" for one year, joined the army at Fishkill on the Hudson and spent the following winter at Danbury, Ct.

In spring of 1780 joined the regiment of Col. Miller and spent the balance of his term of enlistment scouting as far north as West Point and was discharged at expiration of term of service. In March, 1781, he again enlisted and joined the army near West Point in Col. Alex Scammel's regiment, which dropped down the Hudson to Kingsbridge, thence to New Jersey, Philadelphia and Annapolis and finally reached Yorktown in time to participate in the seige and surrender. Thence he followed the fortunes of the army in its long march to Saratoga, thence to Princeton, New Jersey, and West Point, where he was discharged December 23, 1783 without pay and left to travel 300 miles to his home, carrying the musket he had borne through his long service. The old musket was treasured many years in his family and finally presented to the State of Maine by his oldest son, Judge Redington.

Mr. Redington came to Vassalboro in 1784, married Mary, daughter of Nehemiah Getchell, September 2, 1787. Came to Waterville (then Winslow) in 1792 where he died, March 31, 1845. He was buried in Monument Park, where his remains still lie.

Asa Redington was grandfather of Mrs. Appleton A. Plaisted of Waterville.

Simeon Simpson: Simeon Simpson enlisted in Winslow in July, 1782, for three years, in Capt. King's company, Lieut.-Col. Brooks' regiment (the 7th Mass. Line) ; transferred to the 4th Massachusetts Line and was discharged in the State of New York, December 31, 1783. Mr. Simpson was pensioned in 1818.

In a paper dated October 11, 1836, he alleged that he was seventy years old. This would make his birth in 1766, and his age ninety-four at his death, September 24, 1860, though he claimed to be ninety-six.

He was buried in Winslow on the home farm, now owned by the Lockwood Company. Before this article goes to press, his remains will have been removed, with those of his family, to Pine Grove Cemetery.

Jonathan Soule: Appears with rank of *private* on muster and pay roll of Captain Calvin Partridge's company, Colonel John Cushing's regiment, for service at Rhode Island. Enlisted, September 23, 1776. Time of service, one month, twenty-eight days. Vol. 3, p. 62.

Jonathan Soule: Appears with rank of *private* on muster and pay roll of Captain James Harlow's company, Col. Ezra Wood's regiment, raised for eight months to guard the passage of North river. Enlisted, June 5, 1778. Time of service, eight months, four days. Vol. 20, p. 8.

He died January 6, 1832, aged eighty-four, and was buried in the old Elm street cemetery, and in 1875 removed to Pine Grove Cemetery.

Lot Sturtevant: Was born in Wareham, Mass., July 25, 1759. He was the second son of Joseph and Mary (Gibbs) Sturtevant. Joseph was the son of Moses, son of Samuel, son of Samuel, who was at Plymouth, Mass., as early as May, 1642. His affidavit, on file in the land office at the State House, Augusta, gives the following:

"Lot Sturtevant of Waterville, June 15, 1835, seventy-five years old and upwards, enlisted at Wareham, Mass., 1777, for three years in Capt. Josh Eddy's company, Gen. Bradford's regiment, Massachusetts Line. Served his full time and was honorably discharged at West Point in 1780. United States pensioner. Land certificate granted April 19, 1835."

It cannot be ascertained when he came to Waterville, but it must have been before 1790, for his eldest son, Zenas, was born here in November, 1790, and the succeeding children, seven in all, were born here prior to 1806. He married Elizabeth Bessie, who was born October 3, 1764 or 5, and died January 13, 1833, aged sixty-eight. Lot Sturtevant died at Waterville, June 4, 1848, aged eighty-eight, at the home of Reward Sturtevant.

His farm was one of the "Ten Lots" of which he was the original settler and proprietor. Here he lived, reared his family, and was buried in the cemetery one mile north of Fairfield Center on the Pishons Ferry Road.

Richard Sweetzer: Of North Yarmouth is credited with service as a private in Capt. Noyes' company, Col. Phinney's regiment of eight months' men with the army at the siege of Boston in 1775.

Mr. Sweetzer lived here in 1840 with David Parker; was a pensioner and ninety years of age. When he came here, when he died and where he was buried are unknown.

Philip Thayer: Supposed to have been born near Attleboro, Mass. and enlisted from there. Came to Berwick after the war and finally drifted "down east" to Waterville (now Oakland) died and was buried in the old cemetery there. No other record.

Obadiah Williams: Was a surgeon in Gen. Starks' regiment at Bunker Hill, and served during the entire Revolutionary War. He came from Epping, N. H., to Waterville (then Winslow) in 1792, and built the first frame house in Waterville, the small one-story house still standing opposite the electric light station at the end of the bridge. The view from this little home of his down the bay and the broad Kennebec must have been very delightful, (since obstructed by the old Dalton house and the factories). Dr. Williams died in 1799, aged forty-nine. He was buried in the old cemetery, now Monument Park, which was then only an open field without fences, and was deeded to the town of Winslow for a burying ground, with certain reservations. When the lines were run to define the boundary on the south side, it was found that Dr. Williams and his wife had been buried outside the cemetery. Their remains were taken up and removed so as to come within the bounds, and when the change was effected, making a public park of the old cemetery, their remains were again moved to Pine Grove Cemetery.

George Young: Was a Revolutionary soldier who came to Waterville (now Oakland) to live, died and was buried there in the old cemetery. Birthplace, date of birth, military record, age and date of death unknown.

Reference is had in Massachusetts military service record to his being commissioned captain of the 5th company, Col. Wheaton's (4th Lincoln county) regiment of Massachusetts militia, in July, 1776, but no service is found credited to him as such.

Note—The writer would acknowledge his indebtedness to C. J. House, Esq., of the Industrial Bureau, Augusta, Me., and E. L. Getchell, Esq., of Harvard University, for valuable research and results in Revolutionary records.

THE WAR OF 1812.

The War of 1812, as is well known grew out of the claim of Great Britain to the right of search of our merchant vessels, and the impressment of American seamen under various pretexts, which culminated in a "State of War," as declared by our National Congress, June 18, 1812, and proclaimed by President Madison, the following day.

The following are the Rosters of the several companies of militia enlisted from Waterville and vicinity for the war, with their service as noted. The residence of the company officers is given while that of the men is not and the records at Augusta and Washington do not give them, but as the Waterville companies were recruited here, the means of transportation at that time primitive and limited, the inference is that they were probably residents of Waterville.

Service from the 14th to 25th September, 1814.

ROLL OF THE FIELD AND STAFF OF LIEUT.-COL. ELNATHAN SHERWIN'S REGIMENT OF MILITIA.

Being the 1st Regiment, 2nd Brigade, 8th Division, in service at Augusta from the 14th to the 25th of September, 1814. This regiment started for the seaboard but was ordered into camp at Augusta to await orders. On the 24th day of September there was a draft from the regiment to fill up the regiment of Lieut.-Col. Ellis Sweet in service at Bath. Those of the regiment not drafted were discharged on the 25th day of September, 1814.

Elnathan Sherwin, Lieut.-Col., Waterville; John Cleaveland, Major, Fairfield; Richard M. Dorr, Major; Ephraim Getchell, Adjutant; Joseph H. Hallett, Or.-Mast., Waterville; Ambrose Howard, Or.-Mast.-Sgt.; Moses Appleton, Surgeon, Winslow; David Wheeler, Paymaster, Waterville; Zedekiah Belknap, Chaplain, Waterville; Moses Healey, Drum-major; Benjamin Foster, Fife-major; Thomas Leeman, Fife-major.

FIELD AND STAFF ROLL

Of Lieut.-Col. Elnathan Sherwin's drafted regiment of militia in service at Wiscasset and Edgecomb from the 24th of September to the 10th of November, 1814.

Elnathan Sherwin, Lieut.-Col., Waterville; Richard M. Dorr, Major; Nathan Stanley, Major, China; Moses Appleton, Surgeon, Winslow; Joseph Bachellor, Surgeon's Mate; Ephraim Getchell, Adjutant; David Wheeler, Paymaster, Waterville; Joseph H. Hallett, Qr.-Master; Charles Haydon, Jr., Sergt.-Major; Benjamin Foster, Qr.-Mast.-Sgt.; David Low, Drum-Major; Thomas Leeman, Fife-Major.

ROLL OF CAPTAIN DEAN BANGS' COMPANY OF ARTILLERY.

In Major Joseph Chandler's Battalion raised in *Waterville* and *Vassalborc* and in service at Augusta waiting orders, from the 12th to the 24th of September, 1814.

Commissioned officers: Dean Bangs, Capt., Waterville; Lemuel Pullen, Lieut., Waterville; Abraham Smith, Lieut., Waterville.

Sergeants: Jabez Dow, Artemus Smith, Levi Moore, Jr., William McFarland.

Corporals: William Marston, Alexander McKechnie, Abiel Moore, James Bragg.

Musicians: Henry Richardson, Reward Sturtevant.

Privates: William Bates, Dennis Blackwell, Ellis Blackwell, William Blish, Andrew Bradford, Martin Bradford, Charles Freeman, Joseph Gulliver, Samuel Hastings, Godfrey Jackson, Joseph Marston, Josiah Merrill, Newall Page, Benjamin Rives, James Shorey, Jeremiah Smith, Joseph Smiley, Jeremiah Tozier, 3, Alvin Trask, Jonathan C. Tozier.

Capt. Dean Bangs was a privateer and a soldier of the American Revolution.

ROLL OF CAPTAIN WILLIAM PULLEN'S COMPANY OF MILITIA.

In Lieut.-Col. Elnathan Sherwin's regiment, raised in Waterville and in service at Augusta from the 14th to the 25th of September, 1814.

William Pullen, Capt., Waterville; Joseph Warren, Lieut., Waterville; Leonard Cornforth, Ensign, Waterville.

Sergeants: Ichabod Smith, Reuben Ricker, Isaiah Hallett, John Hallett.

Corporals: Samuel Merry, James Gilbert, Wiman Shorey, Thomas Stevens.

Musicians: Dexter Pullen, Isaac Gage, Asa Bates.

Privates: Philip Badger, James Burgess, Thomas Bessey, Seth Crowell, Isaiah Crowell, David Coombs, Miller Crowell, John Cobb, Hiram Crowell, Seward Corson, Daniel Duren, Pliny Farrington, Seth Gage, Bryant Gleason, Reuben Gage, Jr., Dennis Gibbs, Timothy B. Hayward, Elijah Hayden, Elisha Hallett, Jr., Josiah M. Hallett, Ebenezer Hussey, John Hussey, Job Harlow, Asa Lewis, Moody Lander, Ivory Low, Abraham Lander, Jr., William Lewis, Jr., William Merryfield, Samuel Merryfield, George Ricker, George Ricker, 2d or Jr., James Rice, Benjamin Stevens, Philander Soule, Isaac Terrill, Leonard Tupper, James White, Cyrus Wheeler, Lorin Wade.

ROLL OF CAPTAIN JOSEPH HITCHINGS' COMPANY OF MILITIA.

In Lieut.-Col. Elnathan Sherwin's regiment raised in Waterville and in service at Augusta from the 14th to the 25th of September, 1814.

Joseph Hitchings, Capt., Waterville; Samuel Webb, Lieut., Waterville; Thomas McFarland, Ensign, Waterville.

Sergeants: Josiah Jacob, Jr., Abraham Morrill, Solomon Berry, Calvin L. Getchell.

Corporals: Abraham Butts, Pelatiah Soule, Simeon Tozer, 2, William Watson.

Musicians: David Low, Lewis Tozier.

Privates: John Bennet, Jonas Blanchard, Columbus Bacon, John Clifford, Richard Clifford, Jacob Cool, Zacheus Foster, Abel Getchell, Joseph Hogden, William Hume, Thomas Parker, Jr., David Parker, William Phillips, David Priest, Arby Penney, Moses Ricker, William Redington, Samuel Redington, Silas Redington, John Stackpole, Benjamin Smith, William Smith, George Soule, Daniel Soule, Sullivan Soule, Richard Sweetzer, William Sweetzer, William Tozer, Stephen Tozer.

ROLL OF CAPT. CHILD'S COMPANY FROM WINSLOW.

James L. Child, Capt.; Washington Heald, Lieut.; Wm. Getchell, Ensign.

Sergeants: Wm. Harvey, James Heald, Joel Crosby, Abraham Bean.

Corporals: Alvin Blackwell, Richard V. Hayden, Simeon Heald, Elisha Ellis.

Privates: Charles Hayden, Jr., Hernend C. Barton, Samuel Bates, Clark Drummond, James Fife, Wm. Fletcher, Asa Getchell, Zipheroe Howard, Joseph Heald, Daniel Libby, Wm. Pollard, Geo. Pillsbury, Thos. J. Pressey, Daniel Richards, Rufus Rhodes, Ebenezer Richardson, Sam'l Richardson, Adna Reynolds, Wm. Spring, Joseph Swift, Phinehas Small, Jeremiah B. Thompson, Butler Wood, Ephriam Wilson, Jr., Samuel Wilson, Luke Wilson, Wm. Wyman, Benj. Windship, Geo. Abbot, Wentworth Ross, Stephen Getchell, Levi Pollard, Wm. Ham, Frederic R. Paine, John Gould, Nathaniel Dingley, Stephen Abbot.

Amos P. Southard was born and enlisted in Litchfield or Edgecomb. Soon after the war he moved to Winslow, where he lived nearly fifty years, and died in 1870.

An act "Declaring war between Great Britain and her dependencies, and the United States and their Territories" was passed by Congress and signed by the President, June 18, 1812. Treaty of peace was concluded, December 24, 1814, ratification exchanged, February 17, 1815, and proclaimed, February 18, 1815.

From reports of the third auditor of the Treasury Department dated December 12, 1836, (published in Ex. Doc. No. 20, House of Representatives, 24th Congress, 2nd Session,) and February 22, 1858, (published in Ex. Doc. No. 72, House of Representatives, 35th Congress, 1st Session), it appears that the total number of regulars, militia, volunteers and rangers who served the United States at any time during the war of 1812 was 528,274. It is evident that this number represents only the number of enlistments and not the actual number of individuals in service. It is known that many of the men who served during the War of

1812 rendered more than one term, or "tour," of service. But the number of men who served more than one term cannot be ascertained, and it is impossible, therefore, to determine the actual number of individuals in service during that war.

Waterville's most eminent soldier in the War of 1812 was Gen. Eleazer Wheelock Ripley.

Born in Hanover, N. H., April 15, 1782, he was a nephew of President John Wheelock and son of Prof. Sylvanus Ripley, D. D., of Dartmouth, and was graduated at Dartmouth in 1800. He studied law in the office of Hon. Timothy Boutelle, and of his tax assessed in 1809, $2 was tax on his income as a lawyer. He was town agent in 1809 and 1810, was one of the first board of fire wardens elected in 1809, and was chosen by the town as one of the petitioners to the general court to annex Waterville to Somerset county.

May 7, 1810, he was elected by the town its representative to the general court of Massachusetts and was re-elected, May 13, 1811. He was Speaker of the House and was elected Senator in 1812. He became lieutenant-colonel of the 21st Regiment Massachusetts Infantry, March 12, 1812, and just one year later, colonel. He was made brigadier-general, April 15, 1814, and major-general, July 25, 1814. He was wounded in the attack on Toronto but soon after commanded the 2nd Brigade under Gen. Brown on the Niagara frontier. At the battle of Lundy's Lane, after the wounding of Gen. Brown, the command of the army devolved on Gen. Ripley. He was severely wounded in the battle of Niagara but was conspicuous for gallantry in defense of Fort Erie, August 15, 1814. November 3, 1814, by resolution of Congress, he was presented with a gold medal inscribed with the names, "Niagara, Chippewa, Erie." He remained in the U. S. Army until 1820, stationed in Louisiana. He then resigned, practiced law in Louisiana, served in the State Senate, and was a member of Congress from 1835 to 1839. He died in Louisiana, March 2, 1839.

THE AROOSTOOK WAR.

From the close of the War of 1812, the Northwestern boundary of Maine was in dispute till 1839, when the Legislature (of Maine) in private session took measures to drive trespassers from their camps in the valley of the Aroostook river.

The first detachment in charge of a sheriff was captured and taken to jail at Fredericton, N. B., whereupon the Governor of New Brunswick sent word to Governor Fairfield that he had orders to hold the disputed territory by military force and demanded the recall of all militia from the Aroostook.

The people were aroused; the Legislature indignant! Money was voted for the protection of the public lands, and a draft of 10,000 men from the militia was ordered and the men sent at once, through the winter snows to the frontier, where they spent three months near Presque Isle, on the Aroostook.

A company was drafted here and at Fairfield with Samuel Burrill as captain, and on February 25, 1839 joined the 2nd Regiment at Augusta, and marched through deep snow to the frontier.

A peaceful settlement was enforced by this timely occupation and the troops marched home.

A roster of the Waterville-Fairfield company with the names of the Waterville men marked with a star, follows. But one man of this company from Waterville survives, Adrastus Branch.

ROLL OF CAPT. SAMUEL BURRILL'S CO. I OF INFANTRY,

In the detachment of drafted militia of Maine, 2nd Regiment, 1st Brigade, 2nd Division, called into actual service by the State of Maine for the protection of its Northwestern frontier, from the 25th of February to the 19th of April, 1839.

Commissioned officers: Captain, Samuel Burrill, Fairfield; Lieutenant, John J. Emery, Fairfield; Ensign, Charles Cornforth, Waterville.*

Sergeants: James Hasty, Jr.,* Elias C. Hallett,* William Gardner,* William L. Maxwell.*

Corporals: John Bradbury, Ephriam W. Leach, Daniel W. Tinkham,* Thurston H. Tozier.*

Musicians: Josiah Pearl, Silas Richardson.*

Privates: David P. Banks,* Goodwin Bradbury, Walter Burleigh,* Adrastus Branch,* Gersham Boston,* Charles Church, Isaac B. Clifford,* Benjamin F. Corson,* Eben S. Corson,* Charles E. Dillingham,* William Davis,* Briggs H. Emery, 2nd, John Evans,* Joseph Fogg, William Green,* Heman Gibbs, Jr.,* Abisha Higgins,* James Heywood, Moses Healey, Jr.,* James Holmes,* Chancellor Johnson,* Williams Lander,* Theodore McGrath,* George W. Priest,* Granville D. Pullen,* Joseph G. Peavey,* William Peavy,* Joseph Peavy,* John Rines, George Rose,* Joseph Ricker, Jr.,* Ivory Ricker,* William Southwick, Henry A. Shorey,* Hartson Smith,* Peter Sibley, Jr.,* Curtis Tobey, William P. Tozier,* William Woodman,* Charles S. Wyman, James E. Wyman, Sewell Whitcomb,* Thomas Whitcomb,* James Wyman.

Officers' servants: Joshua Ellis, Jr., Capt's.; Thomas J. Emery,* Lieut's.; Oliver Cornforth,* Ensign's.

MEXICAN WAR.

No record has been found on the rolls of the war department of the enlistment of any volunteer soldiers from Waterville for service during the Mexican War, either for volunteer regiments or for the regular army.

The principal recruiting in Maine was at Portland, Bangor, Eastport and Lewiston.

Hiram Cothsan enlisted at Bangor, September 28, 1847, giving his birthplace as Waterville, Maine. He was assigned to Company M, 2nd Artillery, U. S. A., and was discharged therefrom July 19, 1848, by expiration of service, as a musician.

Hostilities began April 24, 1846, with a skirmish which resulted in the capture of Captain Thornton and his party of dragoons by the Mexicans. The act of Congress approved May 13, 1846, declares that "A state of war exists between that government (Mexico) and the United States." Treaty of peace was concluded February 2, 1848, ratifications exchanged May 30, 1848, and proclaimed July 4, 1848.

From a report of the adjutant general, dated December 3, 1849, (published in Ex. Doc. No. 24, House of Representatives, 31st Congress, 1st session), together with certain additions compiled from the official records on file in this office, it appears that the number of regulars and volunteers received into service during the war with Mexico was 101,110.

WAR WITH SPAIN.

From a "Statistical Exhibit of Strength of Volunteer Forces called into Service during the War with Spain," published by the adjutant general's office, December 13, 1899, it appears that the total number of volunteers in service during the war was 223,235. This number includes 453 officers who were also officers in the regular army.

Our representation in this war is as follows:

First Battalion Heavy Artillery.

Avery, Harley E.,	C,	Private.
Barnaby, Alec,	C,	Private,
Barnes, Ernest A.,	C,	Private.
Barry, Richard J., Jr.,	C,	Private.
Bennett, Nelson,	A,	Private.
Butler, Joe,	A,	Private.
Buzzell, Henry E.,	C,	Corporal.
Cabana, Charles L.,	A,	Private.
Chanpagne, Mathias,	C,	Private.
Cone, Augustus,	C,	Private.
Conway, James J.,	A,	Private.
Dutton, James W.,	C,	2d Lieutenant.
Ferguson, William,	C,	Sergeant.
Foster, Ralph H.,	D,	Musician.
Francouer, Joseph,	C,	Private,
Furlong, Richard E.,	C,	Private.
Greenwood, Arthur	A,	Private.
Hall, Fred G.,	D,	Private.
Keniston, Charles W.,	C,	Private.
Latlip, Frank C.,	A,	Private.
Lessor, Edward,	A,	Private.

Libbey, Llewellyn M.,	A,	Private.
McLellan, William J.,	C,	Sergeant.
Merrill, Edmund W.,	C,	Corporal.
Moore, Thomas F.,	A,	Private.
Perry, Frank F.,	A,	Private.
Pooler, David B.,	C,	Private.
Pooler, Fred E.,	A,	Private.
Pooler, Harry,	C,	Private.
Soucier, Oniseme,	C,	Private.
Sterling, William I.,	C,	Corporal.
Thing, Daniel H.,	C,	Private.
Vigue, Joseph,	A,	Private.
Volier, Joseph D.,	C,	Private.
Willette, Edward,	C,	Private.

First Maine Infantry.

Berg, Lars,	L,	Private.
Burgess, Fred E.,	M,	Private.
Dor, George F.,	L,	Private.
Ellis, Walter L.,	B,	Private.
Gilman, Forest J.,	M,	Corporal.
Hewes, Irving R.,	L,	Private.
King, Joseph F.,	H,	Private.
Lidstrom, Axel,	M,	Private.
Pomelow, Trefflin,	Band,	Private.
Pooler, William J.,	M,	Private.
Surman, William J.,	D,	Private.
Winslow, Henry L.,	E,	Private.

PHILIPPINE WAR.

From a "Table Showing the Organization, Service and Strength of the United States Volunteers Authorized by the Act of March 2, 1899," published by the adjutant general's office October 1, 1901, it appears that the total number of volunteers in service during the Philippine Insurrection was 39,178. This number includes 252 officers who were also officers in the regular army.

List of Soldiers of Philippine War from Waterville.

Burgess, private, Co. C., 43rd U. S. Inf.; Butler, Melville, private, Co. B, 43rd U. S. Inf.; Barker, Edwin, private, Co. B, 43rd U. S. Inf.; Besse, Edward H., Q. M. sergeant, 5th U. S. Inf.; Chamberlain, William, private, Co. B, 43rd U. S. Inf.; Doe, George Fred, sergeant, Co. I, 43rd U. S. Inf.; Dutton, J. W., 1st lieutenant, Co. B, 43rd U. S. Inf.; Furlong, Richard E., Jr., private, Co. I, 46th U. S. Inf.; Hawes, Percy W., private, Co. B, 43rd U. S. Inf.; Larkin, Phillip, private, Co. B, 43rd U. S. Inf.; Latlip, Fred, private, Co. B, 43rd U. S. Inf.; McLellan, William J., sergeant, Co. B, 43rd U. S. Inf.; McFarland, Howard, sergeant, Co. B, 43rd U. S. Inf.; Micue, John, private, Co. B, 43rd U. S. Inf.; Micue, Joseph, private, Co. B, 43rd U. S. Inf.; Micue, Gus, private, Co. B, 43rd U. S. Inf.; Morgan, G. A., U. S. Art.; Pomeleau, Trefflie, private, Co. B, 43rd U. S. Inf., (killed in action); Preble, Hallis, musician (band) 43rd U. S. Inf.; Pooler, Barney, private, Co. B, 43rd U. S. Infantry; Quint, Willis, private, Co. B, 43rd U. S. Inf.; Tallouse, Willie, private, Co. H, 43rd U. S. Inf.; Towle, Winfred, private, Co. B, 43rd U. S. Inf.; Wilson, George A., Jr., musician (band) 43rd U. S. Inf.

REGULAR ARMY AND NAVY.

Among the sons of Waterville who have served in the regular army and navy are:

Lieut. Boutelle Noyes, U. S. N., the son of Edwin and Helen (Boutelle) Noyes, was born in Waterville, January 3, 1848. He entered the United States Naval Academy, September 26, 1864, and was graduated with honor in 1868. His first service afloat was on the Guerrier, flag-ship of the South Atlantic Squadron, 1868-69. He was promoted to be Ensign in 1869. He was in the European fleet from 1869-1872, was promoted to be Master in 1870 and commissioned Lieutenant in 1873, which rank he held at his death. From 1873-1877 he was with the South Pacific fleet; was on the training ship Minnesota from 1877 to 1880. In 1881 he was ordered to the Asiatic squadron on board the

Richmond where he met his death by accident, August 29, 1883. His last command was for his men to save themselves while he, looking out for their safety, died at his post of duty. He had previously received honorable mention for saving the lives of seamen at peril to his own. It was in the days of the Civil War when naval service was of utmost value that Boutelle Noyes gave himself to his country. In the days of peace, promotion was slow, but his high ideals, great ability, and faithful performance of duty seemed to assure the highest rank in his profession.

Lieut. Noyes was married, June 25, 1879, to Miss Charlotte Bleecker Luce. Two sons were born to them. Robert Boutelle Noyes and Stephen Henley Noyes. The family home is at Newport, R. I.

John Herbert Philbrick, was born in Waterville, Maine, June 15th, 1853; fitted for college at the Waterville Classical Institute (now Coburn Classical Institute); entered Colby University, (now Colby College), in 1869; graduated in 1873, A. B.; entered West Point Military Academy, July 1, 1873, and served there as a cadet until June 15, 1877, when he was graduated and appointed 2nd Lieutenant in the 11th U. S. Infantry; he was at first stationed at Fort Bennett, and afterwards at Fort Sully, on the western frontier; in 1879 he was ordered to West Point as acting assistant professor of modern languages at the Military Academy; and at the expiration of this assignment he rejoined his regiment at Fort Sully. He was promoted 1st Lieutenant, April 24, 1886, and served as regimental adjutant from December 1, 1889, until the date of his death, July 24, 1890.

Francis Edward Nye, son of Hon. Joshua Nye, was born in Waterville, Maine, August 27, 1847; entered West Point Military Academy in 1865, and was graduated in 1869, being assigned to the 2nd U. S. Cavalry, in which he served four years. At the expiration of this service he resigned and was in business in Augusta, Maine, for twelve years, was then appointed Captain in the Commissary Department, by President Arthur in 1885; was stationed at Fort Monroe for four years; at Washington, D. C., for five years; June 1, 1896, he was commissioned Major, and was stationed at Omaha, Nebraska, for four years, at Chattanooga, Tenn., and Huntsville, Ala., for one year; he was in

San Juan, P. R., for two years, and since that time has been at Vancouver Barracks, Washington. By regular promotion he has attained the rank of Colonel.

Major-General Charles Heywood, Commander of the Marine Corps of the U. S. Army, was a Waterville boy, the son of Lieut. Charles Heywood of the United States Navy, who died at sea. Before he was twenty years old he received a commission in the Marine Corps, April 5, 1858. Before the Civil War he had seen service off the coast of Africa, and off Nicaragua. He was on the Cumberland at Vera Cruz, Mexico, at the outbreak of the war. He commanded the after-gun deck division in the fight between the Merrimac and the Cumberland, and when the latter went down with the flag flying, Capt. Heywood fired the last gun and jumped overboard. "For gallant and meritorious service on this occasion he was brevetted Major and received honorable mentioned from his commander." Afterward he was in command of the guard on the Hartford, Farragut's flagship and, January, 1864, was made fleet marine officer. He was on the Hartford in the battle of Mobile Bay, commanding a division of nine-inch guns. For his part in this action he was commended and brevetted Lieutenant-Colonel. He shared several other engagements and at the close of the war was recommended for advancement five numbers by a special board. During the railroad riot of 1877 he commanded a battalion of marines and was highly commended for the efficiency of his soldiers as well as for his care of them. He received the thanks of the Navy Department. He rendered important service on the Isthmus of Panama in 1885, commanding a force of 1,100 men and keeping the Panama Railroad open in the midst of revolution. He was made Lieutenant-Colonel in 1888 and three years later became Commandant at Washington Barracks. The good work of the marines during the Spanish War and the present superb condition of the force is largely the result of the work of Gen. Heywood, who has inspired the force with his own spirit, perfected its discipline and provided its thorough equipment. At present the Marine Corps enrolls 6,000 men. Gen. Heywood became Brigadier-General in March, 1899, and Major-General in July, 1902. On the latter occasion a very unusual compliment was paid Gen. Heywood.

The Secretary of the Navy, instead of sending the commission by an aid, the usual custom, called in person and presented the commission with words of high appreciation.

Charles Leonard Phillips, was a member of the class of 1881 at Colby University (now Colby College), and for three years took high rank in his class; at the end of his third year he participated in a competitive examination for entrance to the West Point Military Academy and was the successful candidate; he entered the Academy and graduated with his class; was appointed 2nd Lieutenant and has since been promoted 1st Lieutenant and Captain. Colby College conferred upon him the degree of A. M. (out of course).

Otho W. B. Farr, was born February 6, 1871. He entered Colby in 1888 and West Point Military Academy in June, 1889. He was graduated in 1893 and was assigned to the 2nd Artillery, stationed at Fort Preble, Me. Afterward at Fort Warren, Mass., Fort Riley, Kan., and Fort Sheridan, Ill. He served with light battery A, 2nd Artillery, during the Spanish-American War, taking part in the battle before Santiago de Cuba, July, 1898. Promoted to be 1st Lieutenant, March, 1889, and to Captain, July 1, 1901. Served in Cuba from January, 1899 to January, 1902. Capt. Farr is now stationed at Fort Warren, Mass., and is in command of the 77th Co. Coast Artillery.

Alexander Fred. Hammond Yates, son of Mr. and Mrs. A. R. Yates of this city, was born January 11, 1879. He entered the U. S. Naval Academy at Annapolis in September, 1895, and was graduated, January 28, 1899. He served as ensign on the U. S. Ship Detroit during the Spanish-American War, from June 1st to August 23, 1898. In January, 1899, he was ordered to the Asiatic Station, where he has served on the Oregon and Pampanga and has been in command of the Leyte and Arayat until, his three years' cruise being completed, he was ordered to the United States in the summer of 1902 on a furlough.

www.ingramcontent.com/pod-product-compliance
Lightning Source LLC
Chambersburg PA
CBHW070101100426
42743CB00012B/2627